Marco Colombo

Web Development Essentials Practice Exams

A Collection of Questions and Answers to Pass the 030-100 Exam

2022

Copyright © 2022 by Marco Colombo

All rights reserved. This book or any portion thereof may not be reproduced or used in any manner whatsoever without the express written permission of the publisher except for the use of brief quotations in a book review or scholarly journal.

First Printing: 2022

ISBN: 9798352313473

Contents

Acknowledgment 1

Impressum 3

Preface 5

Assessment Test 7

Answers to the Assessment Test 11

Exam Objectives 17

Practice Exam 1 33

Answers to Practice Exam 1 49

Practice Exam 2 65

Answers to Practice Exam 2 83

Practice Exam 3 99

Answers to Practice Exam 3 115

Practice Exam 4 131

Answers to Practice Exam 4 147

Acknowledgment

This year I had the opportunity to take the Beta exam of the Web Development Essentials certification. When I finished I thought: "Why not write a book of exam simulations to help those who want to get this certification?". This is how this book was born and seeing the great enthusiasm of my followers at the idea of its writing, I immediately committed to making it happen. A huge thank you therefore goes to all my readers who support me day after day and encourage me to do more and more. The messages of appreciation for my work make me really happy.

A dutiful thanks goes to the Linux Professional Institute who gave me the opportunity to become an LPI Publishing Partner and to collaborate with them in writing some LPI Learning Materials for their new learning portal.

Last but not least, thanks to all those who have been close to me during the writing of the book and who have supported me in my project with valuable advice.

I hope that this book will be of help to all those who want to take their first steps in the world of web development and that it can become a reference text for those who want to get the Web Development Essentials certification.

Impressum

This publication meets the requirements of the Linux Professional Institute Publishing Partner (LPP) program. Authors, editors and publishers hereby undertake that the present publication covers the stated learning objectives of the exam(s) covered of the version current at the time of publication. These learning objectives are presented in a complete, technically sound manner and in a form suitable for exam preparation. Visit https://learning.lpi.org to learn more about the LPP program and provide feedback on this publication.

Preface

The Linux Professional Institute designed the Web Development Essentials certification to support students in their first steps in software development. The Web Development Essentials certification covers the most important aspects of web development and by the end of the certification program you will understand the basics of HTML, CSS, JavaScript, Node.js, and SQL.

Through this book you will have the opportunity to test your knowledge before taking the actual certification exam. You will find exam objectives identified by the Linux Professional Institute, an assessment test to understand your entry level, and four practice exams to test your web development skills and simulate the final exam. A detailed explanation of each question allows you to see not only the correct answer, but also the general context to which the question refers.

Note that the questions you will find in this book are not brain dumps and that the author of the book does not approve any type of brain dumps.

Assessment Test

1. Given the following function:

   ```
   const my_var = function(a, b) {
     return a ** b;
   }
   ```

   What statement can be used to log the value returned by this function in the browser console?

   A. console.log(my_var.function(2,6));

   B. console.log(function(my_var[2,6]));

   C. console.log(function.my_var >> 2,6);

   D. console.log(my_var(2,6));

2. You want to insert some list items into an ordered list of tasks. Which of the following is a valid element that you can use in your ordered list?

   A. <input> A new list item </input>

   B. <li> A new list item </li>

   C. <it> A new list item </it>

   D. <ins> A new list item </ins>

3. In HTTP version 1.1, which of the following statements about cookies is true?

    A. If a client allows the use of cookies for HTTP communication with a specific server, the **Set-Cookie** field in the HTTP request header contains the cookies that the server has previously sent to the client using the **Cookie** field in the HTTP response header

    B. If a client allows the use of cookies for HTTP communication with a specific server, the **Set-Cookie** field in the HTTP request header contains the cookies that the server has previously sent to the client using the **Send-Cookie** field in the HTTP response header

    C. If a client allows the use of cookies for HTTP communication with a specific server, the **Send-Cookie** field in the HTTP request header contains the cookies that the server has previously sent to the client using the **Cookie** field in the HTTP response header

    D. If a client allows the use of cookies for HTTP communication with a specific server, the **Cookie** field in the HTTP request header contains the cookies that the server has previously sent to the client using the **Set-Cookie** field in the HTTP response header

4. You want to define a file selection field within a **<form>** element so that a user can choose a file from the file system to be uploaded to the server when the form is submitted. Which of the following elements can you use?

    A. <file id="myfile" name="myfile"> Select a file </file>

    B. <input type="file" id="myfile" name="myfile">

    C. <input type="browse" id="myfile" name="myfile"> Select a file </input>

    D. <file type="browse" id="myfile" name="myfile">

5. You want to write a CSS rule that applies to all **<h2>** elements of an HTML page and underlines the text characters. Which of the following rules can you use?

    A. h2 { text-decoration: underline }

    B. .h2 { text-decoration: underline }

    C. #heading { text-decoration: underline }

    D. heading2 { text-decoration: underline }

6. Working with Node.js, you want to install an external module named **foo**. Which of the following commands can you use?

    A. node install foo

    B. node -i foo

    C. npm i foo

    D. js --install foo

    E. node-install foo

7. Using Express, you are writing a route that handles HTTP GET requests to the **/host** path and sends the **host** field in the HTTP request header to the client. Which of the following properties can you use in **res.send()** to accomplish this task? Assume that you have defined a **req** object representing the HTTP request and a **res** object representing the HTTP response.

    A. req.hostheader()

    B. req.http_header.hostname

    C. req.fetch-header('host')

    D. req.headers['host']

8. You want to select all HTML elements in a web page with the class name **special_border** to perfom some action on them. Which of the following instructions can you use? Assume that you are using JavaScript to access the Document Object Model (DOM) elements.

    A. document.selectByClass('.special_border')

    B. document.getElementByClass('special_border')

    C. document.getElementsByClassName('special_border')

    D. document.selectorByClassName('.special_border')

9. Which of the following is an absolute unit? Select three.

    A. px

    B. vw

    C. pt

    D. cm

    E. %

10. Using SQL, you want to extract records that meet a specified condition from a table. How can you accomplish this task? Assume that you are using SQLite as your database.

    A. You can use a **SELECT** statement with the **WHERE** clause

    B. You can use a **SELECT** statement with the **HAVE** clause

    C. You can use a **FIND** statement with the **WHERE** clause

    D. You can use a **FIND** statement with the **HAVE** clause

Answers to the Assessment Test

1. **D - Objective 034.3**

   To invoke a function created with a function expression and stored in a variable, you need to specify the name of the variable, which is used as a function, and the arguments according to its definition. The function in the question, which simply returns the result of raising the first parameter **a** to the power of the second parameter **b**, has no name (it is an anonymous function) and is assigned to the variable named **my_var**. Therefore, to invoke it, you can use **my_var(2,6)** which calls the function with arguments **2** and **6**; the value **2** is assigned to **a**, while the value **6** is assigned to **b** and both will be available within the function like ordinary variables. The function executes its instructions and returns the value **64**, which can then be logged in the browser console using the **console.log()** method. This makes option D the correct answer.

2. **B - Objective 032.2**

   In HTML, the **<li>** element is used to define a list item in ordered (**<ol>**) and unordered (**<ul>**) lists. In ordered lists, you can specify the **value** attribute of **<li>** to indicate the initial value of the item so that subsequent ones increment from that number. Therefore, option B is the correct answer. For completeness, **<input>** is a void element used to specify an input field in a form, **<ins>** is an element used to define a text that has been inserted into a document (it is usually underlined), and **<it>** is an invalid element. Finally, remember that

`<ol>`, `<ul>`, `<li>`, and `<ins>` have a closing tag which is `</ol>`, `</ul>`, `</li>`, and `</ins>` respectively.

3. D - Objective 031.3

An HTTP header is a specific area on each HTTP request and response that contains additional information exchanged by the client and server during their HTTP communication. It consists of case-insensitive names and their corresponding value separated by a colon (:) and is usually invisible to the end user. An HTTP request header contains information about the request, while an HTTP response header contains information about the response. In particular, if a client allows the use of cookies for HTTP communication with a specific server, the **Cookie** field in the HTTP request header contains the cookies that the server has previously sent to the client using the **Set-Cookie** field in the HTTP response header. This makes option D the correct answer. For completeness, remember that multiple **Set-Cookie** fields can be used to send different cookies to the same client.

4. B - Objective 032.4

In HTML, an `<input>` element is used to specify an interactive control for a user interface where a user can enter data. It is a self-closing element and does not have the closing tag. The different types of `<input>` elements that can be displayed depend on the specified **type** attribute. An `<input>` element of type **file** defines a file selection field used to choose a file from the file system that will be uploaded to the server when the form is submitted. To allow selection of multiple files, the **multiple** attribute must be specified (it is a Boolean attribute). Finally, to indicate the types of files the `<input>` field can accept, you need to specify the **accept** attribute (it is a comma-separated list of unique file type identifiers such as **accept=".jpg, .jpeg, .png"**). Therefore, option B is the correct answer. For completeness, **browse** is an invalid value for the **type** attribute of an `<input>` element and `<file>` is an invalid HTML element.

5. A - Objective 033.2

In CSS, selectors are used to select the content you want to style. Specifically, you can use: a type selector which is a selector that matches one or more elements based on the tag name and is specified with the tag name of the element or elements you want to style, an ID selector which is a selector that matches a specific element based on its **id** attribute and is specified with a hash character (**#**) followed by the id of the element you want to style, and a class selector which is a selector that matches one or more elements with a particular **class** attribute and is specified with a period (**.**) followed by the class name of the element or elements you want to style (remember that you can group selectors by separating them with commas). Therefore, option A is the correct answer. For completeness, the selector in option B is used to match all elements with class **h2**, the selector in option C is used to match the element with the **id** attribute set to **heading**, and the selector in option D is not a valid selector.

6. C - Objective 035.1

NPM (originally short for Node Package Manager) is the default package manager for Node.js. It consists of an online repository of packages (the **npm registry**) and a command line interface tool (**npm**) for interacting with this repository. In particular, the **npm install** (or **npm i**) command followed by a module name is used to install the specified module and its dependencies in the **node_modules** directory in the current project directory. This command also adds the specified module to the dependencies of the **package.json** file (the **package-lock.json** file describing the exact dependency tree is updated accordingly). Therefore, option C is the correct answer.

7. D - Objective 035.2

In Express, **req.headers** is the object that contains the HTTP request header. Therefore, you can access the **host** property using **req.headers['host']** or **req.headers.host**, making option D the correct answer. For completeness, the **req.http_header** object does not exist and the **hostheader()** and **fetch-header()** methods are invalid for the **req** object.

8. C - Objective 034.4

The Document Object Model (DOM) is a programming interface for web documents. In the DOM, all HTML elements are defined as objects and the **document** object is the main object representing the web page loaded in the browser. All other objects branch off from it in a tree of objects. DOM methods are the actions that you can perform on the HTML elements and **getElementsByClassName()** is the method used to find elements with a given class name (it can be called on the **document** object to search within the entire document or on a specific element to search only among elements that are descendants of the specified element). You can also specify multiple class names by separating them with white space. Therefore, option C is the correct answer. For completeness, **getElementByClass()**, **selectByClass()**, and **selectorByClassName()** are not valid DOM methods. Finally, remember that **getElementsByClassName()** returns a live collection of elements (an array-like object) that is automatically updated when the underlying document is changed: so be careful when iterating over the returned elements.

9. A, C, D - Objective 033.3

Absolute units are fixed and not relative to anything else. Common units are: **cm** (centimeter), **mm** (millimeter), **in** (inch - 1in = 2.54cm = 96px), **px** (pixel - 1px = 1/96th of 1in), and **pt** (point - 1pt = 1/72 of 1in). Instead, relative units are relative to something else and therefore are not fixed. For example, **vw** is relative to 1% of the viewport width, **vh** is relative to 1% of the viewport height, and **%** (percentage) is relative to the parent element. This makes options A, C, and D the correct answers. For completeness, remember not to leave a white space between the number and the unit (if the value is 0, the unit can be omitted) and that pixels depend on the viewing device (the ratio between pixels and inches varies for example for high resolution screens).

10.A - Objective 035.3

In SQL, the **SELECT** statement is used to query data from one or more tables and the **WHERE** clause allows you to filter records based on one or more conditions. Therefore, option A is the correct answer. For completeness, **FIND** is not a valid SQL statement and the **HAVE** clause does not exist.

Exam Objectives

Topic 031 - Software Development and Web Technologies

031.1 - Software Development Basics (Weight: 1)

Description:

The candidate should be familiar with the most essential concepts of software development and be aware of important programming languages.

Key Knowledge Areas:

- Understand what source code is
- Understand the principles of compilers and interpreters
- Understand the concept of libraries
- Understand the concepts of functional, procedural and object-oriented programming
- Awareness of common features of source code editors and integrated development environments (IDE)
- Awareness of version control systems
- Awareness of software testing
- Awareness of important programming languages (C, C++, C#, Java, JavaScript, Python, PHP)

031.2 - Web Application Architecture (Weight: 2)

Description:

The candidate should understand common standards in web development technology and architecture.

Key Knowledge Areas:

- Understand the principle of client and server computing
- Understand the role of web browsers and be aware of commonly used web browsers
- Understand the role of web servers and application servers
- Understand common web development technologies and standards
- Understand the principles of APIs
- Understand the principle of relational and non-relational (NoSQL) databases
- Awareness of commonly used open source database management systems
- Awareness of REST and GraphQL
- Awareness of single-page applications
- Awareness of web application packaging
- Awareness of WebAssembly
- Awareness of content management systems

Files, terms, and utilities:

- Chrome, Edge, Firefox, Safari, Internet Explorer
- HTML, CSS, JavaScript
- SQLite, MySQL, MariaDB, PostgreSQL

- MongoDB, CouchDB, Redis

031.3 - HTTP Basics (Weight: 3)

Description:

The candidate should be familiar with the basics of HTTP. This includes understanding HTTP headers, content types, caching, and status codes. Furthermore, the candidate should understand the principles of cookies and their role for session handling and be aware of advanced HTTP features.

Key Knowledge Areas:

- Understand HTTP GET and POST methods, status codes, headers and content types
- Understand the difference between static and dynamic content
- Understand HTTP URLs
- Understand how HTTP URLs are mapped to file system paths
- Upload files to a web server's document root
- Understand caching
- Understand cookies
- Awareness of sessions and session hijacking
- Awareness of commonly used HTTP servers
- Awareness of HTTPS and TLS
- Awareness of web sockets
- Awareness of virtual hosts
- Awareness of common HTTP servers
- Awareness of network bandwidth and latency requirements and limitations

Files, terms, and utilities:

- GET, POST
- 200, 301, 302, 401, 403, 404, 500
- Apache HTTP Server ("httpd"), NGINX

Topic 032 - HTML Document Markup

032.1 - HTML Document Anatomy (Weight: 2)

Description:

The candidate should understand the anatomy and syntax of an HTML document. This includes creating basic HTML documents.

Key Knowledge Areas:

- Create a simple HTML document
- Understand the role of HTML
- Understand the HTML skeleton
- Understand the HTML syntax (tags, attributes, comments)
- Understand the HTML head
- Understand meta tags
- Understand character encoding

Files, terms, and utilities:

- <!DOCTYPE html>
- <html>
- <head>
- <body>

- \<meta\>, including the charset (UTF-8), name and content attributes

032.2 - HTML Semantics and Document Hierarchy (Weight: 2)

Description:

The candidate should be able to create HTML documents with a semantic structure.

Key Knowledge Areas:

- Create markup for contents in an HTML document
- Understand the hierarchical HTML text structure
- Differentiate between block and inline HTML elements
- Understand important semantic structural HTML elements

Files, terms, and utilities:

- \<h1\>, \<h2\>, \<h3\>, \<h4\>, \<h5\>, \<h6\>
- \<p\>
- \<ul\>, \<ol\>, \<li\>
- \<dl\>, \<dt\>, \<dd\>
- \<pre\>
- \<blockquote\>
- \<strong\>, \<em\>, \<code\>
- \<b\>, \<i\>, \<u\>
- \<span\>
- \<div\>
- \<main\>, \<header\>, \<nav\>, \<section\>, \<footer\>

032.3 - HTML References and Embedded Resources (Weight: 2)

Description:

The candidate should be able to link an HTML document with other documents and embed external content, such as images, videos and audio in an HTML document.

Key Knowledge Areas:

- Create links to external resources and page anchors
- Add images to HTML documents
- Understand key properties of common media file formats, including PNG, JPG and SVG
- Awareness of iframes

Files, terms, and utilities:

- id attribute
- <a>, including the href and target (_blank, _self, _parent, _top) attributes
- <img>, including the src and alt attributes

032.4 - HTML Forms (Weight: 2)

Description:

The candidate should be able to create simple HTML forms containing input elements of various types.

Key Knowledge Areas:

- Create simple HTML forms
- Understand HTML form methods

- Understand HTML input elements and types

Files, terms, and utilities:

- `<form>`, including the method (get, post), action, and enctype attributes
- `<input>`, including the type (text, email, password, number, date, file, range, radio, checkbox, hidden) attribute
- `<button>`, including the type (submit, reset, hidden, button) attribute
- `<textarea>`
- common form element attributes (name, value, id)
- `<label>`, including the for attribute

Topic 033 - CSS Content Styling

033.1 - CSS Basics (Weight: 1)

Description:

The candidate should understand the various ways to style an HTML document using CSS. This includes the structure and syntax of CSS rules.

Key Knowledge Areas:

- Embedding CSS within an HTML document
- Understand the CSS syntax
- Add comments to CSS
- Awareness of accessibility features and requirements

Files, terms, and utilities:

- HTML style and type (text/css) attributes

- <style>
- <link>, including the rel (stylesheet), type (text/css) and src attributes
- ;
- /*,*/

033.2 - CSS Selectors and Style Application (Weight: 3)

Description:

The candidate should be able to use selectors in CSS and understand how CSS rules are applied to elements within an HTML document.

Key Knowledge Areas:

- Use selectors to apply CSS rules to elements
- Understand CSS pseudo-classes
- Understand rule order and precedence in CSS
- Understand inheritance in CSS

Files, terms, and utilities:

- element; .class; #id
- a, b; a.class; a b;
- :hover, :focus
- !important

033.3 - CSS Styling (Weight: 2)

Description:

The candidate should use CSS to add simple styles to the elements of an HTML document.

Key Knowledge Areas:

- Understand fundamental CSS properties
- Understand units commonly used in CSS

Files, terms, and utilities:

- px, %, em, rem, vw, vh
- color, background, background-*, font, font-*, text-*, list-style, line-height

033.4 - CSS Box Model and Layout (Weight: 2)

Description:

The candidate should understand the CSS box model. This includes defining the position of elements on a website. Additionally, the candidate should understand the document flow.

Key Knowledge Areas:

- Define the dimension, position and alignment of elements in a CSS layout
- Specify how text flows around other elements
- Understand the document flow
- Awareness of the CSS grid
- Awareness of responsive web design
- Awareness of CSS media queries

Files, terms, and utilities:

- width, height, padding, padding-*, margin, margin-*, border, border-*
- top, left, right, bottom

- display: block | inline | flex | inline-flex | none
- position: static | relative | absolute | fixed | sticky
- float: left | right | none
- clear: left | right | both | none

Topic 034 - JavaScript Programming

034.1 - JavaScript Execution and Syntax (Weight: 1)

Description:

The candidate should be able to execute JavaScript files and inline code from an HTML document and understand basic JavaScript syntax.

Key Knowledge Areas:

- Run JavaScript within an HTML document
- Understand the JavaScript syntax
- Add comments to JavaScript code
- Access the JavaScript console
- Write to the JavaScript console

Files, terms, and utilities:

- <script>, including the type (text/javascript) and src attributes
- ;
- //, /* */
- console.log

034.2 - JavaScript Data Structures (Weight: 3)

Description:

The candidate should be able to use variables in JavaScript code. This includes understanding values and data types. Furthermore, the candidate should understand assignment operators and type conversion and be aware of variable scope.

Key Knowledge Areas:

- Define and use variables and constants
- Understand data types
- Understand type conversion/coercion
- Understand arrays and objects
- Awareness of the variable scope

Files, terms, and utilities:

- =, +, -, *, /, %, --, ++, +=, -=, *=, /=
- var, let, const
- boolean, number, string, symbol
- array, object
- undefined, null, NaN

034.3 - JavaScript Control Structures and Functions (Weight: 4)

Description:

The candidate should be able to use control structures in JavaScript code. This includes using comparison operators. Furthermore, the candidate should be able to write simple functions and understand function parameters and return values.

Key Knowledge Areas:

- Understand truthy and falsy values
- Understand comparison operators
- Understand the difference between loose and strict comparison
- Use conditionals
- Use loops
- Define custom functions

Files, terms, and utilities:

- if, else if, else
- switch, case, break
- for, while, break, continue
- function, return
- ==, !=, <, <=, >, >=
- ===, !==

034.4 - JavaScript Manipulation of Website Content and Styling (Weight: 2)

Description:

The candidate should understand the HTML DOM. This includes manipulating HTML elements and CSS properties through the DOM using JavaScript as well as using DOM events in simple scenarios.

Key Knowledge Areas:

- Understand the concept and structure of the DOM

- Change the contents and properties of HTML elements through the DOM
- Change the CSS styling of HTML elements through the DOM
- Trigger JavaScript functions from HTML elements

Files, terms, and utilities:

- document.getElementById(), document.getElementsByClassName(), document.getElementsByTagName(), document.querySelector(), document.querySelectorAll()
- innerHTML, setAttribute(), removeAttribute() properties and methods of DOM elements
- classList, classList.add(), classList.remove(), classList.toggle() properties and methods of DOM elements
- onClick, onMouseOver, onMouseOut attributes of HTML elements

Topic 035 - NodeJS Server Programming

035.1 - NodeJS Basics (Weight: 1)

Description:

The candidate should understand the basics of NodeJS. This includes running a local development server as well as understanding the concept of NPM modules.

Key Knowledge Areas:

- Understand the concepts of Node.js
- Run a NodeJS application
- Install NPM packages

Files, terms, and utilities:

- node [file.js]
- npm init
- npm install [module_name]
- package.json
- node_modules

035.2 - NodeJS Express Basics (Weight: 4)

Description:

The candidate should be able to create a simple dynamic website with the Express web framework. This includes defining simple Express routes as well as serving dynamic files through the template engine EJS.

Key Knowledge Areas:

- Define routes to static files and EJS templates
- Serve static files through Express
- Serve EJS templates through Express
- Create simple, non-nested EJS templates
- Use the request object to access HTTP GET and POST parameters and process data submitted through HTML forms
- Awareness of user input validation
- Awareness of cross-site Scripting (XSS)
- Awareness of cross-site request forgery (CSRF)

Files, terms, and utilities:

- express and body-parser node module
- Express app object

- app.get(), app.post()
- res.query, res.body
- ejs node module
- res.render()
- <% ... %>, <%= ... %>, <%# ... %>, <%- ... %>
- views/

035.3 - SQL Basics (Weight: 3)

Description:

The candidate should be able to create individual tables in an SQLite database and add, modify and delete data using SQL. Furthermore, the candidate should be able to retrieve data from individual tables and execute SQL queries from NodeJS. This does not include referencing or combining data between multiple tables.

Key Knowledge Areas:

- Establish a database connection from NodeJS
- Retrieve data from the database in NodeJS
- Execute SQL queries from NodeJS
- Create simple SQL queries excluding joins
- Understand primary keys
- Escape variables used in SQL queries
- Awareness of SQL injections

Files, terms, and utilities:

- sqlite3 NPM module

- Database.run(), Database.close(), Database.all(), Database.get(), Database.each()
- CREATE TABLE
- INSERT, SELECT, DELETE, UPDATE

Practice Exam 1

1. You have a paragraph defined as follows: **<p> My paragraph </p>**. Which of the following attributes can you use to change the style of this element (such as color, size, and font)?

    A. class

    B. css

    C. css-style

    D. style

2. Which of the following statements about cookies is true?

    A. Cookies can introduce potential security and privacy issues as they can be stolen from a client and used to impersonate the client they were stolen from

    B. Cookies can introduce potential security vulnerabilities as they can contain executable code and can be used to transfer viruses or malware to a computer

    C. Cookies are absolutely safe and do not introduce any kind of vulnerability from the point of view of privacy and security

    D. Cookies can only introduce limited vulnerabilities as they are only used to record users' browsing habits and are unable to save login information and to preserve sessions

3. Given the following **<iframe>** element:

   ```
   <iframe   src="my_iframe.html"   name="my_iframe"   width="500"
   height="400">

   <p>Unsupported browser</p>

   </iframe>
   ```

   What HTML element can you use to create a hyperlink to a web page named **newpage.html** that opens in the iframe specified above when the user clicks on the hyperlink?

   A. <a target="newpage.html" load="my_iframe"> Go to a new HTML Page </a>

   B. <a href="newpage.html" target="my_iframe"> Go to a new HTML Page </a>

   C. <a src="newpage.html" load="my_iframe" target="_IFRAME"> Go to a new HTML Page </a>

   D. <a src="newpage.html" target="IFRAME: my_iframe"> Go to a new HTML Page </a>

4. You want to select all **<h2>** elements in a web page to perform some action on them and assign the resulting list to the variable named **elements**. Which of the following assignment statements can you use? Assume that you are using JavaScript to access the Document Object Model (DOM) elements.

   A. const elements = document.querySelector("h2");

   B. const elements = document.querySelectorAll("h2");

   C. const elements = document.getElementsByTag("h2");

   D. const elements = document.getAllElementsByTagName("h2");

5. An HTML document normally has a **<head>** element which is a container for the metadata of the document and a **<body>** element which is a container for all the contents of the document. Which of the following elements encloses **<head>** and **<body>** and gives with them the basic structure of an HTML document?

   A. <p>

   B. <root>

   C. <html>

   D. <h>

6. You want to define a label for the following **<input>** element:

   ```
   <input type="text" id="id_input" name="name_input">
   ```

   Which of the following HTML elements can you use?

   A. <label for="name_input"> Username </label>

   B. <label bind="name_input"> Username </label>

   C. <label for="id_input"> Username </label>

   D. <label bind="id_input"> Username </label>

7. Which of the following statements about Node.js is true?

   A. Node.js is a runtime environment to execute client-side JavaScript code within the web browser

   B. Node.js uses Multi-Threaded Request/Response architecture

   C. Node.js is asynchronous and uses event driven programming

   D. Node.js uses a blocking approach for I/O processing

8. Given the following excerpt of JavaScript code:

```
var a = 10;
var b = a--;
console.log(b);
```

What is the value logged in the browser console? Just write the number.

9. What statement can be used to invoke the following function, created with a function declaration, with arguments **5** and **3**, and log its return value to the browser console?

```
function min(a,b)
{
  if(a>b) { return b; } else { return a; }
}
```

A. console.log(function.min(5,3));

B. console.log(function min(5,3));

C. console.log(min(5,3));

D. console.log(min(a: 5,b: 3));

10. You want to insert some JavaScript code directly in your HTML page. Within which tags do you need to insert your JavaScript code?

A. Between the <javascript> and </javascript> tags

B. Between the <code> and </code> tags

C. Between the <script> and </script> tags

D. Between the <ext-code> and </ext-code> tags

11. Using Express and Embedded JavaScript (EJS), you want to insert the escaped contents of the variable named **my_var** into a template file during the rendering process. Which of the following EJS tags can you use?

    A. <%- my_var %>

    B. <%= my_var %>

    C. ${my_var}

    D. %{my_var}%

12. Given the following CSS rules:

    ```
    p#par_a {
      background-color: blue
    }
    p {
      background-color: yellow
    }
    ```

    What will be the background color of the paragraph with **id** set to **par_a**? Just write the color name in lowercase. Assume that only these two CSS rules apply to your HTML page.

13. You want to make the text oblique for all elements that match a specified selector. Which of the following CSS properties can you use in your CSS rule?

    A. font-type: oblique;

    B. font-style: oblique;

    C. font-line: oblique;

    D. font-family: oblique;

14. Which of the following is a phrase tag that you can use to add semantic importance to snippets of text? Select two.

    A. <code>

    B. <b>

    C. <em>

    D. <u>

    E. <i>

15. You want to create an object named **company** with the **name** and **number** attributes to store the business name of a company and the number of its employees. Which of the following declarations can you use?

    A. var company = [name("xyz"), number(150)];

    B. var company = { name["xyz"], number[150] };

    C. var company = { name: "xyz", number: 150 };

    D. var company: company.name="xyz", company.number=150;

16. Which of the following is a core attribute that can be used with all HTML elements? Select three.

    A. id

    B. title

    C. label

    D. class

    E. charset

17. You want to group some inline elements for styling purposes using a generic inline container. Which of the following HTML elements can you use?

    A. <span>

    B. <div>

    C. <group>

    D. <inline-div>

    E. <in-grp>

18. You want to write the number of elements of an array named **LinuxDistributions** to the browser console. Which of the following instructions can you use?

    A. console.log(LinuxDistributions,length());

    B. console.log(length:LinuxDistributions);

    C. console.log(length(LinuxDistributions));

    D. console.log(LinuxDistributions.length);

19. Which of the following statements about HTTP GET and POST methods is true? Select two.

    A. The GET method is used to send data to the server to create or update a resource

    B. POST requests remain in the browser history

    C. GET requests can be cached

    D. GET requests cannot be bookmarked

    E. POST requests have no data length restrictions

20. Given the following CSS rule:

```
body {
  background-image: url("my_image.jpg");
  background-repeat: no-repeat;
  background-position: center;
  background-attachment: fixed;
}
```

How can you rewrite it using a single shorthand property?

A. body { background: url("my_image.jpg"), center, no-repeat, fixed; }

B. body { background: url("my_image.jpg") center no-repeat fixed; }

C. body { bg: url("my_image.jpg") no-repeat fixed center; }

D. body { bg: no-repeat, url("my_image.jpg"), fixed, center; }

21. Using Express, you have successfully inserted a row using an **INSERT INTO** statement. Which of the following properties of the **this** object of the callback function contains the value of the last inserted row ID? Assume that you have loaded the **sqlite3** module, defined a constant named **db** to perform all database operations, and executed the **INSERT INTO** statement with **db.run()**.

A. pKEY

B. KEY

C. rowID

D. lastID

22. Which of the following statements about an IDE is true?

    A. An Integrated Database Engine (IDE) is a software program used in web development to connect multiple relational or non-relational database management systems to a web application

    B. An Improved Disability Experience (IDE) is a software program that facilitates the browsing experience for people with disabilities

    C. An Integrated Development Environment (IDE) is a software program that facilitates application development by combining all the tools a developer needs, such as a source code editor, a debugger, and build automation tools, into a single graphical user interface (GUI)

    D. An Interconnected Desktop Environment (IDE) is a desktop environment containing a web server and a client application that connects to it

23. Media queries are used in responsive web design. Which of the following statements is true?

    A. Media queries use the **@expression** CSS at-rule to create different layouts for different devices and different media types

    B. Media queries use the **@media** CSS at-rule to create different layouts for different devices and different media types

    C. Media queries use the **@test** CSS at-rule to create different layouts for different devices and different media types

    D. Media queries use the **@query** CSS at-rule to create different layouts for different devices and different media types

24. You want to write a CSS rule that applies to all <a> elements of an HTML page with the **class** attribute set to **nounderline**. Which of the following selectors can you use?

    A. a.class=nounderline

    B. .nounderline

    C. a.nounderline

    D. a.class==nounderline

25. You want to write a CSS rule that makes the text red for all <h4>, <h5>, and <h6> elements. Which of the following rules can you use?

    A. h4, h5, h6 { color: red }

    B. h4; h5; h6 { color: red }

    C. h(4,5,6) { color: red }

    D. h4 && h5 && h6 { color: red }

26. Using JavaScript, you want to perfom some instructions if the value of the **var** variable is between **0** and **10** inclusive. Which of the following conditions can you use in your **if** statement?

    A. var >= 0 && var <= 10

    B. var >= 0 || var <= 10

    C. var >= 0 !& var <= 10

    D. var >= 0 !| var <= 10

    E. var >= 0 & var <= 10

    F. var >= 0 | var <= 10

27. Complete the following statement in your Node.js application:

```
const express = _____ ('express')
```

Assume that you have already installed the **express** module and now want to use it.

28. In web development, what does the term PWA mean?

    A. PHP Web Access - a PHP login script that can be used to provide authentication for your web pages

    B. Powered Web Apps - very sophisticated web applications that reside on remote servers that must always be connected to the Internet to avoid loss of productivity

    C. Progressive Web Apps - web applications built with common web technologies that look and act like mobile apps

    D. Plugin for Web Authentication - a plugin that allows you to securely access a web application without requiring a username or password, but using devices such as USB Keys or fingerprint scanners

29. You have developed an Express application with a route that handles HTTP GET requests to the **/res** path and now you want to test that it works. Which of the following commands can you use? Assume you have defined a server with name **myserver** listening on port **8080**.

    A. curl http://myserver:8080/res

    B. http --request get http://myserver:8080/res

    C. curl http://myserver/res:8080

    D. http --request get http://myserver/res -p 8080

    E. ndget --url http://myserver/res -p 8080

30. Which of the following is a valid **while** statement? Assume that you have already defined a variable **i** with the value 0.

    A. while (i=0;i < 10;i++) {

    if(i % 2 != 0) { console.log(i); }

    }

    B. { if(i % 2 != 0) { console.log(i); }

    while (i < 10)}

    C. while (i < 10; i++) {

    if(i % 2 != 0) { console.log(i); }

    }

    D. while (i < 10) {

    if(i % 2 != 0) { console.log(i); }

    i++;

    }

31. Which of the following statements about the CSS **display** property is true? Select two.

    A. If set to **block**, it displays an element as a block element

    B. If set to **bl-flex**, it displays an element as a block-level flex container

    C. If set to **flex-level**, it displays an element as an inline-level flex container

    D. If set to **inline-level**, it displays an element as an inline element

    E. If set to **flex**, it displays an element as a block-level flex container

32. You want to retrieve all the columns of the table named **animals**. Which of the following SQL statements can you use? Assume that you are using SQLite as your database.

    A. SELECT * IN animals;

    B. SELECT ALL WHERE animals;

    C. SELECT * FROM animals;

    D. SELECT ALL animals;

33. You want to embed an image named **foo.jpg** in an HTML page. Which of the following elements can you use? Assume the image file is in the same folder as your HTML page.

    A. <img href="foo.jpg" width="300" height="400"> Description of foo </img>

    B. <img url="foo.jpg" width="300" height="400"> Description of foo </img>

    C. <img source="foo.jpg" alt="Description of foo" width="300" height="400">

    D. <img src="foo.jpg" alt="Description of foo" width="300" height="400">

34. Which of the following statements about standard HTTP status codes is true?

    A. Codes starting with 1 are success codes

    B. Codes starting with 5 are redirection codes

    C. Codes starting with 2 are server error codes

    D. Codes starting with 4 are client error codes

35. Which of the following statements about Embedded JavaScript (EJS) is true? Select two. Assume you have already loaded the **express** module and created an Express application named **app**.

   A. You can set EJS as the view engine for the Express application using **app.set('view engine', 'ejs')**

   B. You can set EJS as the view engine for the Express application using **app.set('ejs', 'template engine')**

   C. By default, **views** is the folder in the application root directory where the template files are located

   D. By default, **public** is the folder in the application root directory where the template files are located

   E. By default, **guest** is the folder in the application root directory where the template files are located

36. Using JavaScript, you want to terminate the execution of a loop if a particular condition is met. Which of the following instructions can you use?

   A. clear;

   B. stop;

   C. exit;

   D. continue;

   E. break;

37. Complete the following SQL **UPDATE** statement:

   UPDATE employees ____ jobtitle = 'General Manager' WHERE id = 150;

   Assume that you are using SQLite as your database. Just write the missing word in uppercase.

38. Which of the following programming languages is normally used in front-end development to make web pages dynamic thus allowing users to interact with them?

   A. HTML

   B. JavaScript

   C. CSS

   D. Cassandra

39. You want to change the inner HTML markup code of a selected element. Which of the following DOM properties do you need to change? Assume that you are using JavaScript to access the Document Object Model (DOM) elements.

   A. innerHTML

   B. text

   C. HTMLcontent

   D. innerContent

40. You have an HTML form with two **<input>** elements, one of type **text** and the other of type **password**. Which of the following attributes can you use to specify that these elements must be filled before submitting the form?

   A. required

   B. mandatory

   C. set

   D. load

Answers to Practice Exam 1

1. **D - Objective 033.1**

   If you want to change the style of an HTML element, you can use the **style** attribute directly in the element's opening tag. This attribute can be used with all HTML elements and can contain one or more CSS properties. Therefore, option D is the correct answer. For completeness, the **class** attribute is used to specify one or more class names for an HTML document, while the **css** and **css-style** attributes do not exist. Finally remember that properties specified in the **style** attribute override properties defined within a **<style>** element or in an external style sheet.

2. **A - Objective 031.3**

   Cookies are small data files that are saved on a computer by web sites visited by a user. They are used for many purposes such as to identify users and save their preferences, save login information, save product information, record users' browsing habits, preserve sessions, and so on. As a result, cookies can introduce potential security and privacy issues for a client if an attacker gets hold of them: in fact, they can be used to impersonate the original client from which they were stolen when making a request to the server. Cross-site scripting (XSS) and cross-site request forgery (CSRF) are two common techniques a malicious user can use to steal cookies from a client. To avoid these potential vulnerabilities, it may be useful to implement protection mechanisms that allow you to have a secure control over session and cookie management. Finally, although cookies may represent potential vulnerabilities, they cannot cause any harm to a computer: they are just small data files and cannot contain executable code and cannot transfer viruses or malware to a computer.

3. B - Objective 032.3

In HTML, the **<a>** element is used to define a hyperlink. In particular, the **href** attribute specifies the destination of the link (the URL that the hyperlink points to) and the **target** attribute specifies where to display the URL. If you want to open the web page indicated in the **href** attribute in a specific **<iframe>** element, you need to set the **target** attribute to the **name** attribute of the **<iframe>**. Therefore, option B is the correct answer. For completeness, the **<a>** element does not have the **load** and **src** attributes.

4. B - Objective 034.4

The DOM method named **querySelector()** returns the first element that matches the specified CSS selector or null if no match is found, while the DOM method named **querySelectorAll()** returns a static list of elements that match the specified CSS selector. In both cases, a valid CSS selector string must be specified within the round brackets. Therefore, to select all **<h2>** elements in a web page, you can use the following assignment statement: **const elements = document.querySelectorAll("h2");**. This makes option B the correct answer. For completeness, **getAllElementsByTagName()** and **getElementsByTag()** and are not valid DOM methods.

5. C - Objective 032.1

The **<html>** element contains all other HTML elements and is known as the root element. It contains **<head>** and **<body>**, thus enclosing the entire HTML document, and gives with them the basic structure of an HTML document. Only the **doctype** declaration is not inside

`<html>`; this declaration is the first line of code and specifies the browser which version of HTML is used in the document (for HTML 5 `<!DOCTYPE html>`). Therefore, option C is the correct answer. For completeness, the `<p>` element is used to specify a paragraph, while the `<root>` and `<h>` elements do not exist. Remember that the `<head>` element is a container for the document metadata which is not displayed when the page is loaded and that the `<body>` element is a container for all the contents of the document. Also remember that `<html>`, `<head>`, and `<body>` have a closing tag, which is `</html>`, `</head>`, and `</body>` respectively.

6. C - Objective 032.4

In HTML, the `<label>` element is used to define a label for an item in a user interface such as a single line text field. Specifically, to set a label for a form element, the **for** attribute of `<label>` must be the same as the **id** attribute of the related element. Therefore, to bind a label to the `<input>` element specified in the question with **id** set to **id_input**, you need to set the **for** attribute of the `<label>` element to **id_input**. This makes option C the correct answer. For completeness, the **bind** attribute of `<label>` does not exist. Finally, remember that you can achieve the same goal by nesting the `<input>` element directly inside the `<label>` element (in this case the association is implicit and you do not need to use the **for** and **id** attributes).

7. C - Objective 035.1

Node.js is a back-end JavaScript runtime environment that allows you to execute server-side JavaScript. Because it is built on top of the V8 JavaScript engine, you can use JavaScript outside of the web browser. Node.js is open source and cross platform and allows developers to use the same language (JavaScript) for both front-end and back-end development. Node.js uses the Single Threaded Event Loop Model architecture to handle multiple client requests: a Node.js application runs using the event loop, the core component that allows you to run one process at a time. Therefore, Node.js operates asynchronously and in a non-blocking way for I/O processing using event driven programming. This makes option C the correct answer. For completeness, remember that although Node.js allows you to create highly scalable and very fast applications, it is not suitable for compute-intensive tasks.

8. **10 - Objective 034.2**

    In JavaScript, the **var** statement is used to declare a function-scoped or globally-scoped variable. Therefore, the code in the question creates a globally-scoped variable named **a** with value **10**; it then assigns the value of **a** to a new globally-scoped variable named **b** and finally decreases the value of **a** by one. As a result, **a** will have value **9**, while **b** will have value **10**.

9. **C - Objective 034.3**

    To invoke a function created with a function declaration, you need to specify the name of the function and its arguments according to its definition. The function in the question, which simply returns the minimum of two numbers, has the name **min** and two parameters: **a** and **b**. Therefore, to invoke it with arguments **5** and **3**, you can use **min(5,3)**; **5** is assigned to **a** and **3** is assigned to **b**. The function executes its instructions and returns the value **3**, which can then be logged in the browser console using **console.log()**. This makes option C the correct answer.

10. **C - Objective 034.1**

    The JavaScript code is placed between the **<script>** and **</script>** tags, and the position of the **<script>** element within the HTML page determines when the code is executed. However, it is customary to insert the **<script>** element at the end of the HTML **<body>** so that the script is the last thing that is executed or within the **<head>**

section so that the script is executed before parsing the HTML **<body>**. Therefore, option C is the correct answer. For completeness, the **<code>** element is used to specify a computer code snippet, while the **<javascript>** and **<ext-code>** elements do not exist. Finally, remember that the **type** attribute of **<script>** is used to specify the type of the script and its value is by default **application/javascript**.

11. B - Objective 035.2

In Embedded JavaScript (EJS), a template file has specific tags for inserting dynamic content. In particular, the **<%= var %>** tag is used to insert the escaped value of the **var** variable in a template file during the rendering process (more precisely, **var** is a property of the object passed as a parameter to the **render()** method of the HTTP response object). Since the contents of the variable are escaped, special characters such as < and > are replaced with their HTML codes when inserting the variable value in the template file (for < and >, you will find **<** and **>** in the source code of the displayed HTML page); if you want to insert the unescaped value of the variable into the template file, you can use **<%- var %>** instead. This makes option B the correct answer. For completeness, remember that it is a good practice to escape content to avoid executing malicious JavaScript code that can be exploited for cross-site scripting (XSS) attacks.

12. blue - Objective 033.2

In CSS, if an element matches two or more rules, the rule of the selector with the highest specificity will be applied to that element. The priority order is: inline styles (highest priority), ids, classes, and elements (lowest priority). If an element matches two or more equally specific rules, the last rule will be applied to that element. Finally, if you want a CSS property targeting an HTML element to take precedence over all other declarations of the same CSS property targeting the same HTML element, you can add the **!important** keyword after that CSS property. As a result, the blue color is applied to the text since the

ID selector has a higher priority than the type selector. For completeness, remember that in the case of complex selectors, you need to calculate the specificity of the selectors with appropriate rules, but in the simplest cases (such as those of the Web Development Essentials certification) just remember the priority order and the rules mentioned above.

13. B - Objective 033.3

The **font-style** property is used to specify the font style of a text. Common values for this property are: **normal**, which is the default, to use a normal font style, **italic** to use an italic font style, and **oblique** to use an oblique font style. Therefore, option B is the correct answer. For completeness, the **font-family** property is used to specify one or more specific or generic font family names, while the **font-type** and **font-line** properties do not exist.

14. A, C - Objective 032.2

In HTML, phrase tags are used to change the look of the text while also adding semantic importance. The most common phrase tags are: **<strong>** which is used to give more importance to the text (content is typically displayed in bold), **<em>** which is used to emphasize the text (content is typically displayed in italic), **<mark>** which is used to mark the text in yellow, **<code>** which is used to specify a computer code snippet, **<kbd>** which is used to indicate that a content is a user input from the keyboard, **<var>** which is used to indicate that the content is a variable, and **<samp>** which is used to specify a sample output from a program or script. Instead, presentation tags only affect the presentation of the text and the most common are: **<b>** which is used to make text bold, **<i>** which is used to italicize text, and **<u>** which is used to underline text. Therefore, options A and C are the correct answers. For completeness, remember that although some phrase and presentation tags allow you to display text in the same way, it is best to use a phrase tag as it adds semantic importance to the text, is interpreted by screen readers, and is used by search engines. Also remember that all elements mentioned above have a closing tag.

15. C - Objective 034.2

In JavaScript, objects are used to store more complex entities (the **Object** class is one of the JavaScript's data types). An object is a collection of comma-separated properties enclosed in curly brackets (**{}**), each of which associates a name with a value (name and value are separated by colons). If the value of a property is a function, the property is known as a method. An object property is accessible using **ObjectName.PropertyName**, **ObjectName["PropertyName"]** or **ObjectName['PropertyName']**, both for reading and for assigning new values. Instead, an object method is accessible using **ObjectName.MethodName()**. Therefore, option C is the correct answer.

16. A, B, D - Objective 032.1

Attributes are used to specify additional information about HTML elements. They are set in the opening tag and are in the form **ProperyName="Value"** (both single or double quotes can be used). In particular, core (or global) attributes are attributes that can be used with all HTML elements. Common global attributes are: **id** which is used to specify a unique identifier for an element, **class** which is used to specify one or more classes (defined in a style sheet) for an element, **style** which is used to specify a CSS style for an element, **lang** which is used to specify the language of the element's content, **hidden** which is uses to specify to browsers whether or not to display an element (it's a boolean), and **title** which is used to specify additional details for an element (it is usually displayed as a tooltip when the user's cursor is over the element). Therefore, options A, B, and D are the correct answers. For completeness, the **label** attribute, used to add a short label, is specific to some HTML elements, while the **charset** attribute does not exist.

17. A - Objective 032.2

The **<span>** element is a generic inline-level container, typically used to group inline elements for styling purposes. Therefore, option A is the correct answer. For completeness, the **<div>** element is a block-level container for other HTML elements and is normally used to define sections in an HTML document, while the **<group>**, **<inline-div>**, and **<in-grp>** elements do not exist. Finally, remember that **<span>** and **<div>** have no effect on the layout until they are styled in some way with CSS and that they have a closing tag.

18. D - Objective 034.2

In JavaScript, the **length** property of an array returns the number of elements in the array (**arrayName.length**). Therefore, option D is the correct answer.

19. C, E - Objective 031.3

GET and POST are two common HTTP methods: GET is used to request data from the server, while POST is used to send data to the server to create or update a resource (it is usually used to add a resource, for example when submitting an HTML form or when uploading data to the server). HTTP GET requests include all data in clear text in the URL and therefore can be cached, remain in the browser history, can be bookmarked, and should never be used to send passwords or other sensitive information. Since the data is in the URL, there is also a limit to the amount of information that can be sent. Instead, HTTP POST requests include all data in the message body of the HTTP request and therefore cannot be cached, do not remain in the browser history, cannot be bookmarked, have no data length restrictions, and can be used to send sensitive information (POST is safer than GET). This makes options C and E the correct answers.

Answers to Practice Exam 1

20. B - Objective 033.3

The **background** property is a shorthand for all other **background-*** properties. Therefore, you can use this property to rewrite the CSS rule in the question by combining **background-image**, **background-repeat**, **background-position**, and **background-attachment** into one property (remember that individual properties are not separated by commas). This makes option B the correct answer. For completeness, the **background-image** property is used to set one or more background images for an element (e.g. via URL), the **background-repeat** property is used to set how a background image is repeated (e.g. **repeat-x**, **repeat-y**, or **no-repeat**), the **background-position** property is used to set the initial position of a background image (e.g. **left bottom**, **center**, **30% 20%**, or **50%**), the **background-attachment** property is used to set whether the position of a background image is fixed or scrolls with the page (e.g. **scroll**, **fixed**, or **local**), and the **bg** property does not exist. Remember that, using **background**, if you want to specify the size of a background image with the **background-size** property, you must separate it from **background-position** with a **/**. Also remember that you can specify multiple background layers separated by commas, each of which has its own properties; in this scenario the **background-color** property used to set a background color must be included in the last layer.

21. D - Objective 035.3

When you successfully execute an **INSERT INTO** statement with **db.run()**, the **this** object of the callback function contains the **lastID** property which stores the value of the last inserted row ID (**this.lastID**). Therefore, option D is the correct answer.

22. C - Objective 031.1

An Integrated Development Environment (IDE) is a software program that facilitates application development. It combines all the tools developers need for their daily programming tasks, such as a source code editor, a debugger, and build automation tools, into a single graphical user interface (GUI). Each IDE has its own features and tools that can also help developers save time and reduce errors. Popular IDEs are **Eclipse**, **Visual Studio**, **Lazarus**, and **Xcode**. This makes option C the correct answer.

23. B - Objective 033.4

Media queries are a key aspect in responsive web design as they allow you check various conditions such as screen resolution, orientation, viewport size, and media type. They use the **@media** CSS at-rule to create different layouts depending on these conditions, thus creating different styles for different devices (e.g. desktop, tablets, and mobile phones) and for different media types (e.g. printers and screens). You can create different media queries according to your needs; just remember that you need to specify the correct media type (e.g. **screen** for computer screens, tablets, and mobile phones and **print** for printers and devices intended to reproduce a printed display) and/or one or more test expressions involving so-called media features (e.g. **orientation** for the orientation of the viewport and **min-width** for the minimum width of the display area). This makes option B the correct answer.

24. C - Objective 033.2

In CSS, the **TypeElement.ClassName** selector is used to match elements of type **TypeElement** with the **class** attribute set to **ClassName**. Therefore, the **a.nounderline** selector matches all **<a>** elements with the **class** attribute set to **nounderline**, making option C the correct answer. For completeness, the **.nounderline** selector matches all elements with the **class** attribute set to **nounderline** regardless of their type, while **a.class=nounderline** and **a.class==nounderline** are invalid selectors.

25. A - Objective 033.2

According to the explanation of question 5 of the Assessment Test, you can group selectors by separating them with commas. Therefore, to group the type selectors for the **<h4>**, **<h5>**, and **<h6>** elements, you can use **h4, h5, h6**. This makes option A the correct answer.

26. A - Objective 034.3

If you want to test multiple conditions in an **if** statement, you need to combine them using logical operators. In particular, with the logical AND operator (**&&**), the entire expression returns **true** if all individual expressions return **true**, while with the logical OR operator (**||**) the entire expression returns **true** if one of the individual expressions returns **true**. This makes option A the correct answer. Finally, remember that you can also use the logical NOT operator (**!**) which reverses the logical state of the expression (from **true** to **false** and vice versa).

27. require - Objective 035.2

Express.js (or simply Express) is a popular web framework for Node.js. Once installed, you can load it into your Node.js application using the **require** keyword (actually, any previously installed module can be loaded with **require**).

28. C - Objective 031.2

Progressive Web Apps (PWAs) are web applications built with common web technologies that look and act like mobile apps. They are initially perceived as normal web sites but progressively behave like mobile apps. Therefore, PWAs combine the best of web and mobile apps: they can be accessed through a web browser by searching for them via a search engine query, but they can also offer features typical of mobile apps such as speed, push notifications, and the ability to work offline and be accessible from the home screen, thus improving user experience and performance over traditional web sites. Finally, remember that PWAs are cross-platform and can optionally be published on common app stores. This makes option C the correct answer.

29.A - Objective 035.2

Curl is a command line tool used to transfer data to or from a server, allowing you to make HTTP requests such as GET and POST to a server, retrieve HTTP headers, upload files, and much more. It supports several protocols including HTTP and HTTPS and, if followed by the URL without any options (the simplest form), makes an HTTP GET request to the target URL. Therefore, you can use the command **curl http://myserver:8080/res** to make a GET request to the **res** path and output the response body, thus verifying that the route is working correctly (note that the path is specified after the port). This makes option A the correct answer. For completeness, the **http** and **ndget** commands do not exist.

30.D - Objective 034.3

In JavaScript, the **while** loop is used to execute a series of lines of code repetitively as long as an expression is **true**. The syntax to use is: **while (expression) { //code to run at each iteration }**. Therefore, the valid **while** statement is the one in option D which is the correct answer. For completeness, the loop specified in the question is used to log the odd numbers from 0 to 10 in the browser console. The expression **i < 10** is tested (**i** is initialized to 0 before the loop) and, as long as it is **true**, the code within the curly brackets is executed: if **i** is an odd number, it is logged in the browser console and then **i** is incremented by one. At each iteration the expression is checked with the new value of **i** and when **i** equals 10 the loop is ended (the result of the expression is **false**).

31. A, E - Objective 033.4

In CSS, the **display** property is used to specify how an element will be displayed. Some common values are: **inline** which is used to display an element as an inline element, **block** which is used to display an element as a block element, **flex** which is used to display an element as a block-level flex container, **inline-flex** which is used to display an element as an inline-level flex container, and **none** which is used to make an element completely disappear. Therefore, options A and E are the correct answers. For completeness, remember that a flex container is used to better structure the layout of a page, aligning and distributing the space between its items according to the flexbox model, mainly for responsive web design.

32. C - Objective 035.3

In SQL, the **SELECT** statement is used to query data from one or more tables. In its basic form, after **SELECT** you need to specify the list of comma-separated columns to be returned by the query and the **FROM** clause followed by the source table from which to get the data. If you want the query to return all columns in the table, you can use an asterisk (*****) instead of specifying the column names. Therefore, option C is the correct answer.

33. D - Objective 032.3

In HTML, the **<img>** element is used to embed an image in an HTML page. Common attributes for **<img>** are: **src** which is required and contains the path to the image to embed, **alt** which specifies a textual description of the image that is shown if the image cannot be displayed for various reasons such as text-only browsers and network problems, and which is read by screen readers (it is therefore very useful for accessibility), **height** which specifies the height in pixels of the image, and **width** which specifies the width in pixels of the image. Finally, remember that **<img>** is a void element and does not have a closing tag. This makes option D the correct answer. For completeness, the **href**, **url**, and **source** attributes do not exist for the **<img>** element.

34. D - Objective 031.3

HTTP status codes are three-digit code numbers issued by a server in response to a request from a client that concisely specify to the client how the server interpreted and handled the request. They are delivered in the HTTP response header and are grouped into five classes. The first digit of the status code defines the response class, while the other two digits specify the type of response under a given class. A short text description (the Reason Phrase) is usually provided after the status code to specify its meaning. Codes starting with 1 (1XX) are informational codes indicating that the request has been received and understood and that the process continues. Codes starting with 2 (2XX) are success codes indicating that the request has been successfully received, understood, and accepted. Codes starting with 3 (3XX) are redirection codes indicating that the client may take additional action to complete the request. Codes starting with 4 (4XX) are client error codes indicating that the request cannot be fulfilled due to an error from the client. Codes starting with 5 (5XX) are server error codes indicating that the server encountered an error and cannot process a valid request. Based on the above, option D is the correct answer.

35. A, C - Objective 035.2

Embedded JavaScript (EJS) is one of the most popular template engines used by Node.js that allows you to generate HTML markup with plain JavaScript. In simple terms, EJS replaces the JavaScript code embedded in a template file with the actual values and transforms the template file into an HTML file to be sent to the client. To set EJS as the view engine for your Express application named **app**, you need to specify **app.set('view engine', 'ejs')** in your application file. By default, **views** is the folder in the application root directory where you need to store your template files. This makes options A and C the correct answers.

36. E - Objective 034.3

In a JavaScript loop, the **continue** instruction is used to terminate the execution of statements in the current iteration of the loop and start a new iteration, while the **break** instruction is used to terminate the current loop (it jumps out of the loop on the first instruction after the loop). Therefore, option E is the correct answer. For completeness, the **exit**, **stop**, and **clear** instructions do not exist in JavaScript.

37. SET - Objective 035.3

In SQL, the **UPDATE** statement is used to update an existing record in a specified table. The syntax to use is: **UPDATE TableName SET Column1 = Value1, Column2 = Value2, ... ColumnN = ValueN WHERE SearchCondition;**. The **WHERE** clause is optional and indicates the rows in the table (**TableName**) whose columns (**Column1**, **Column2**, ... **ColumnN**) need to be updated with the new values (**Value1**, **Value2**, ... **ValueN**). Finally, note that if you don't use the **WHERE** clause, all the rows in the table will be updated. Therefore, the missing word is **SET**.

38. B - Objective 031.2

Front-end development refers to the creation of web sites and web applications that users interact with and are rendered on the client-side. The three main languages used for front-end development are: **HTML** (HyperText Markup Language) which is used to define the structure and content of web sites, **CSS** (Cascading Style Sheets) which is used to apply styles to web pages, and **JavaScrip**t which is the scripting language used to make web pages dynamic allowing users to interact with them. Therefore, option B is the correct answer. For completeness, **Cassandra** is a common non-relational database.

39. A - Objective 034.4

DOM properties are values of HTML elements that can be set or changed. Specifically, the **innerHTML** property is used to set or get the inner HTML markup code of an element. This makes option A the correct answer. For completeness, **HTMLcontent**, **text**, and **innerContent** are not valid DOM properties.

40. A - Objective 032.4

The **required** attribute is used to specify that an **<input>** element must have a value before submitting the form. It is a Boolean attribute and is supported by both **<input>** elements of type **text** and **password** (it also works with many other types such as **date**, **checkbox**, **radio**, and **file**). Therefore, option A is the correct answer. For completeness, the **mandatory**, **set**, and **load** attributes do not exist for an **<input>** element.

Practice Exam 2

1. Which of the following statements about the **<title>** element is true? Select two.

    A. It specifies the most important heading of the HTML document

    B. It is defined in the **<body>** section

    C. It is the suggested name for the bookmark when the page is added to favorites

    D. It specifies the title of the HTML document and is displayed in the title bar of the web browser or in the page tab.

    E. It is purely indicative and is not important for search engine optimization (SEO)

2. You are writing a CSS rule that makes the text red for all elements that match a specified selector. Which of the following CSS properties can you use in your rule? Select two.

    A. color: FF0000;

    B. color: rgb(FF,0,0);

    C. color: red;

    D. color: rgb(255,0,0);

    E. color: red=FF, green=00, blue=00;

3. Which of the following is a valid HTML element? Select two.

    A. <h7> This is a heading </h7>

    B. <h4> This is a heading </h4>

    C. <p> This is a paragraph </p>

    D. <paragraph value="This is a paragraph">

    E. <heading type="h2" value="This is a heading">

4. You want to create an array of numbers and strings. Which of the following declarations can you use?

    A. var my_array : { 1, "mum", "dad", 45, 8 };

    B. var my_array = [1, "mum", "dad", 45, 8];

    C. var my_array == [1; "mum"; "dad"; 45; 8];

    D. var my_array = 1, "mum", "dad", 45, 8;

    E. It is an invalid declaration because the values stored in an array must be of the same primitive data type

5. You want to write the **Upgrading** message to the browser console followed by the variable named **app** which contains the name of the application you are upgrading. Which of the following instructions can you use?

    A. console.print("Upgrading", app);

    B. console.log("Upgrading", app);

    C. message.writeline("Upgrading", app);

    D. message.display("Upgrading", app)

6. Which of the following represents an ordered list of two items in alphabetical order with lowercase letters starting with **d**?

   A. <ol type="lower" start="d">

      <li> First Item </li>

      <li> Second Item </li>

   </ol>

   B. <ol sort="al" start="d" lower>

      <li> First Item </li>

      <li> Second Item </li>

   </ol>

   C. <ol type="a" start="4">

      <li> First Item </li>

      <li> Second Item </li>

   </ol>

   D. <ol sort="al" start="4" lower>

      <li> First Item </li>

      <li> Second Item </li>

   </ol>

7. Which of the following is a version control system?

   A. Git

   B. NGINX

   C. Redis

   D. SQL

8. Given the following excerpt of JavaScript code:

```
var a = 5;
if (true) {
    let b = a;
}
console.log(b);
```

What is logged in the browser console?

A. 5

B. 0

C. Uncaught SyntaxError: Identifier 'b' has already been declared

D. Uncaught ReferenceError: b is not defined

9. Which of the following is a relational database?

A. MongoDB

B. CouchDB

C. Cassandra

D. SQLite

10. Complete the following route that handles HTTP POST requests to the site root. Assume you have already loaded the **express** module and created an Express application named **app**.

```
app.post('_____', function (req, res) {
    res.send('Post Method OK');
})
```

11. Given the following HTML code:

    ```
    <p id="par_a" class="cl_a"> My first paragraph </p>
    <p id="par_b" class="cl_b"> My second paragraph </p>
    <p id="par_c" class="cl_a"> My third paragraph </p>
    ```

    Which of the following CSS rules can you use to bold only the first paragraph text?

    A. .cl_a { font-weight: bold }

    B. #par_a { font-weight: bold }

    C. p { font-weight: bold }

    D. par_a { font-weight: bold }

    E. par_a, cl_a { font-weight: bold }

    F. cl_a { font-weight: bold }

12. Using **npm**, what is the effect of the following command? Assume that you only have a **package.json** file in the current project directory.

    ```
    npm install
    ```

    A. The command installs all modules in the **npm registry**

    B. The command installs the default Node.js modules which are defined in the **default.conf** file in the directory where Node.js is installed

    C. The command installs all modules that are listed as **dependencies** and **devDependencies** in **package.json**

    D. It is an invalid command; you need to specify the name of the module you want to install

13. You want to make the text larger than the parent element text for all elements that match a specified selector. Which of the following CSS properties can you use in your CSS rule?

    A. font-size: larger;

    B. font-size: bigger;

    C. font-rsize: x-large;

    D. font-rsize: x-parent;

14. You want to place an <img> element on the left side of its <div> container so that the paragraph text within <div> wraps around it. Which of the following properties can you use in the CSS rule for the <img> element?

    A. flow: left-overlap;

    B. float: left;

    C. flow-control: left-overlap;

    D. overlap: left;

15. You want to write a CSS rule that applies to all elements of an HTML page that have both **cl_a** and **cl_b** classes. Which of the following selectors can you use?

    A. .(cl_a,cl_b)

    B. .(cl_a cl_b)

    C. .cl_a && .cl_b

    D. .cl_a.cl_b

16. Using Express, you want to set up a directory named **public** to serve static files located in the same directory of your Node.js application. Which of the following lines do you need to include in your application? Assume you have already loaded the **express** module and created an Express application named **app**.

    A. express.use('public')

    B. app.use(express.static('public'))

    C. app.static('public')

    D. app.load('public', express.static)

17. What is the standard port for HTTPS version 1.1?

    A. 25 TCP

    B. 21 TCP

    C. 443 TCP

    D. 143 TCP

18. Given the following CSS rules:

```
h1 {
 background-color: red !important
}
h1 {
 background-color: blue
}
```

What will the background color of the `<h1>` elements be? Just write the color name in lowercase. Assume that only these two CSS rules apply to your HTML page.

19. Using Express, you want to access the route parameter named **id** that you specify in the URL of your HTTP GET request. Which of the following properties can you use within the route handler function? Assume that you have defined a **req** object representing the HTTP request and a **res** object representing the HTTP response.

    A. req.object.id

    B. req.arguments.id

    C. req.arguments[0]

    D. req.params.id

20. Given the following **<input>** element and its corresponding label:

    ```
    <label for="username">Username:</label>
    <input type="text" id="username" name="username">
    ```

    Which of the following statements is true?

    A. You can provide an example value for the **<input>** element using the **placeholder** attribute, while you can provide an initial value for the **<input>** element using the **value** attribute

    B. You can provide an example value for the **<input>** element using the **sample** attribute, while you can provide an initial value for the **<input>** element using the **default** attribute

    C. You can provide an example value for the **<input>** element using the **initial** attribute, while you can provide an initial value for the **<input>** element using the **default** attribute

    D. You can provide an example value for the **<input>** element using the **sample** attribute, while you can provide an initial value for the **<input>** element using the **value** attribute

21. You want to define two radio buttons in a **<form>** element that represent the **YES** and **NO** options with their label. Which of the following HTML elements can you use? Assume the two radio buttons share the same radio group.

   A. <input type="radio" id="opt_yes" name="opt_yes" group="yes_no" value="YES">

   <label for="opt_yes">YES</label>

   <input type="radio" id="opt_no" name="opt_no" group="yes_no" value="NO">

   <label for="opt_no">NO</label>

   B. <input type="radio" id="opt_yes" name="opt_yes_no" value="YES">

   <label for="opt_yes">YES</label>

   <input type="radio" id="opt_no" name="opt_yes_no" value="NO">

   <label for="opt_no">NO</label>

   C. <input type="radio-group" id="opt_yes" value="YES">

   <label for="opt_yes">YES</label>

   <input type="radio-group" id="opt_no" value="NO">

   <label for="opt_no">NO</label>

   D. <input type="radio-group" id="opt_yes" group="yes_no" value="YES">

   <label for="opt_yes">YES</label>

   <input type="radio-group" id="opt_no" group="yes_no" value="NO">

   <label for="opt_no">NO</label>

22. Which of the following statements about function declarations and function expressions is true? Select two.

   A. The function name can be omitted in functions created with a function declaration

   B. The function name can be omitted in functions created with a function expression

   C. Functions created with a function declaration can be invoked before or after their initialization

   D. Functions created with a function expression can be invoked only before their initialization

   E. Functions created with a function declaration can be invoked only after their initialization

23. Given the following excerpt of JavaScript code:

```
var a = "100";
var b = 100;
var c = 0;


if ( a === b ) {
    c = 3;
} else {
    c = 2;
}

console.log(c);
```

What is logged in the browser console? Just write the number.

24. Using Express, you are writing a route that handles HTTP POST requests to the **sign** path and sends the contents of the **full_name** field in the request body to the client. Which of the following properties can you use in **res.send()** to accomplish this task? Assume that you have defined a **req** object representing the HTTP request and a **res** object representing the HTTP response.

   A. req.body.full_name

   B. req.full_name

   C. req.body-arguments.full_name

   D. req.data.full_name

   E. req.body.data.full_name

25. You have selected all **<h1>** elements in a web page using:

   const elements = document.querySelectorAll("h1");

   Which of the following **for** loops can you use to add the class named **main** to each of the selected elements?

   A. for (element of elements) { element.addClass('main'); }

   B. for (element of elements) { element.classList.add('main'); }

   C. for (let i=0; i<elements.length; i++) {
      elements[i].classAdd('main');
      }

   D. for (let i=0; i<elements.length; i++) {
      elements[i].addClassList('main');
      }

   E. for (element of elements) { element.addToClassList('main'); }

26. You want to use an external style sheet named **custom_styles.css** to style your HTML page. How can you accomplish this task? Suppose the external style sheet is in the same location as the HTML page.

   A. You can add the line **<css href="custom_styles.css"> My custom CSS </css>** in the **<head>** section of your HTML page

   B. You can add the line **<link href="custom_styles.css" rel="stylesheet"> My custom CSS </link>** in the **<head>** section of your HTML page

   C. You can add the line **<link href="custom_styles.css" rel="stylesheet">** in the **<head>** section of your HTML page

   D. You can add the line **<css href="custom_styles.css" rel="stylesheet">** in the **<head>** section of your HTML page

27. Given the following **<p>** elements in a web page:

   ```
   <p id="id_a"> First Paragraph </p>
   <p id="id_b"> Second Paragraph </p>
   <p id="id_c"> Third Paragraph </p>
   ```

   How can you change the inner HTML markup code of the second paragraph to **New Text**?

   A. id_b.selectElementsById().innerHTML = "New Text";

   B. document.querySelectorById("id_b").innerHTML = "New Text";

   C. document.getElementById("id_b").innerHTML = "New Text";

   D. document.selectElementsById("id_b").innerHTML = "New Text";

   E. id_b.querySelectorById().innerHTML = "New Text";

28. Using Express, you want to insert one row into a SQLite table. Which of the following methods can you use? Assume that you have already loaded the **sqlite3** module and defined a constant named **db** to perform all database operations.

    A. db.run()

    B. db.execute()

    C. db.insert()

    D. db.insertINTO()

29. Given the following **<h3>** element:

    <h3 id="id_c"> A Level 3 Heading </h3>

    How can you create a hyperlink on the same page pointing to this **<h3>** element?

    A. <a href="id_c" internal> Go to Lever 3 Heading </a>

    B. <a internal="id_c"> Go to Lever 3 Heading </a>

    C. <a target="#id_c"> Go to Lever 3 Heading </a>

    D. <a href="#id_c"> Go to Lever 3 Heading </a>

30. In HTTP version 1.1, which of the following fields in the HTTP request header specifies to the server which content types, expressed as MIME types, the client accepts for the response?

    A. Expect

    B. Accept

    C. Media-Type

    D. Requested-Type

31. You want to insert the metadata of an HTML page, describing the content of the document. Which of the following elements can you use?

    A. <meta type="description"> Page Description </meta>

    B. <meta name="description"> Page Description </meta>

    C. <meta name="description" content="Page Description">

    D. <meta type="description" name="Page Description">

32. What is the meaning of the 403 status code?

    A. Forbidden - The client does not have the rights to access the content

    B. Bad Syntax - The server cannot process the request due to an apparent error on the client side such as malformed request syntax

    C. Request Timeout - The client request exceeded the time that the server was prepared to wait

    D. Internal Server Error - The server has encountered an unexpected situation that it does not know how to handle

33. Which of the following is a common programming language for back-end development? Select three.

    A. HTML

    B. Ruby

    C. PHP

    D. CSS

    E. JavaScript

34. Using JavaScript, you want to write all the items of the array named **colors** in the browser console. Which of the following **for** loops can you use?

    A. for(let i = 0; i < colors.length; i++) do {console.log(colors[i]);}

    B. for(i < colors.length; let i = 0; i++) do {console.log(colors[i]);} done

    C. for(let i=0; i < colors.length) { console.log(colors[i]); i++; }

    D. for(let i = 0; i < colors.length; i++) { console.log(colors[i]); }

35. Which of the following is a valid keyword that you can use for the **target** attribute of the <a> element? Select two.

    A. _window

    B. _self

    C. _high

    D. _tab

    E. _parent

36. Which of the following is a valid SQL **INSERT INTO** statement? Assume that the **employees** table has two columns: **code** of type **INTEGER** and **name** of type **VARCHAR(50)**. Also assume that you are using SQLite as your database.

    A. INSERT INTO employees (code, name) SET (1000, 'foobar');

    B. INSERT INTO employees (code, name) SET (1000, foobar);

    C. INSERT INTO employees (code, name) VALUES (1000, 'foobar');

    D. INSERT INTO employees (code, name) VALUES (1000, foobar);

37. Using CSS, which of the following is not a valid value for the **position** property? Select two.

    A. relative

    B. sticky

    C. anchored

    D. static

    E. no-offset

38. Which of the following is a valid function created with a function expression?

    A. var conc <= function(str1, str2) { return str1 + " " + str2; };

    B. var conc = function(str1, str2) { return str1 + " " + str2; };

    C. functexpr conc(str1, str2) { return str1 + " " + str2; };

    D. functionExpression => conc(str1, str2) { return str1 + " " + str2; }

39. Using Express, you have successfully deleted some rows using a **DELETE** statement. Which of the following properties of the **this** object of the callback function contains the numbers of rows deleted? Assume that you have loaded the **sqlite3** module, defined a constant named **db** to perform all database operations, and executed the **DELETE** statement with **db.run()**.

    A. changes

    B. lines

    C. rows

    D. numbers

40. You have an object named **song** with three properties: **title**, **singer**, and **year**. How can you log the value of these properties in the browser console?

   A. console.log("Title:", title, "Singer:", singer, "Year:", year);

   B. console.log("Title:", song.title, "Singer:", song.singer, "Year:", song.year);

   C. console.log("Title: " + song[title] + "Singer: " + song[singer] + "Year: " + song[year]);

   D. console.log("Title: " + song(title) + "Singer: " + song(singer) + "Year: " + song(year));

Answers to Practice Exam 2

1. **C, D - Objective 032.1**

   The **<title>** element is used to specify the title of the HTML document and is displayed in the title bar of the web browser or in the page tab. It also provides the suggested name for the bookmark when the page is added to favorites, appears as a clickable headline in search engine results, and is used by search engine algorithms, making it very important for search engine optimization (SEO). The **<title>** element is required in all HTML documents, is defined in the **<head>** section, and must be unique; its closing tag is **</title>**. Therefore, options C and D are the correct answers.

2. **C, D - Objective 033.3**

   The **color** property is used to specify the color of the text. In CSS, a color can be specified in many ways, including the color name, the RGB color value, and the hexadecimal color value. RGB color values follow the syntax **rgb(red,green,blue)** where each color component (**red**, **green**, and **blue**) defines the intensity of the color and is an eight-bit binary number (an integer from **0** to **255**) or a percentage value (from **0%** to **100%**). Hexadecimal color values are defined like this: **#RRGGBB** where each color component (**RR** for red, **GG** for green, and **BB** for blue) is a two-digit hexadecimal value between **00** and **FF** (**00** corresponds to **0** and **FF** corresponds to **255**) and if a component has two identical digits, the second can be omitted. Therefore, to use the color red, you can specify the keyword **red**, the RGB value

rgb(255,0,0), or the hexadecimal value **#FF0000** (the red component is set to the highest value, while the other components are set to zero). This makes options C and D the correct answers. For completeness, remember that color names and hexadecimal color values are not case sensitive and that you can also specify transparency by adding two additional digits between **00** and **FF** for hexadecimal notation or by using **rgba(red,green,blue,alpha_channel)** where **alpha_channel** is number between **0** (fully transparent) and **1** (fully opaque).

3. **B, C - Objective 032.2**

   In HTML, the **<p>** element is used to specify a paragraph, while the **<h1>**, **<h2>**, **<h3>**, **<h4>**, **<h5>**, and **<h6>** elements are used to specify a heading from the most important (**<h1>**) to least important (**<h6>**). The hierarchy and importance of the headings can be seen from the size of the text; so **<h1>** is the heading with larger text, while **<h6>** is the heading with smaller text. **<p>**, **<h1>**, **<h2>**, **<h3>**, **<h4>**, **<h5>**, and **<h6>** have a closing tag, which is **</p>**, **</h1>**, **</h2>**, **</h3>**, **</h4>**, **</h5>**, and **</h6>** respectively. This makes options B and C the correct answers. For completeness, the **<h7>**, **<paragraph>**, and **<heading>** elements do not exist.

4. **B - Objective 034.2**

   An array is a variable that can hold many values. The syntax for declaring an array is **var arrayName = [item1, item2, item3 ... itemN];** (actually, you can also use **const** or **let** instead of **var**). Values stored in an array do not need to be of the same primitive data type. This makes option B the correct answer. Finally, remember that a declaration can span multiple lines.

5. **B - Objective 034.1**

   The JavaScript **console.log()** method is used to print any message (e.g. a string or variable) to the browser console and is commonly used for debugging purposes. This makes option B the correct answer. For completeness, the **message.display()**, **message.writeline()**, and **console.print()** methods do not exist. Finally, remember that the browser console, in addition to the messages sent with **console.log()**, also shows errors and warnings and can be used to execute JavaScript code for testing purposes.

6. C - Objective 032.2

In HTML, the **<ol>** element is used to define an ordered list, and each item of the list is defined by the **<li>** element. Specifically, you can use the following attributes for **<ol>**: **type** to specify the numbering type (**1** for decimal numbers which is the default value, **a** for lowercase letters, **A** for uppercase letters, **i** for lowercase roman numerals, and **I** for uppercase roman numerals), **start** to specify the value of the first item (it is always an integer), and **reversed** to specify whether the items are in reverse/descending order (it is a Boolean attribute). Therefore, option C is the correct answer. For completeness, **lower** is an invalid value for the **type** attribute, **d** is an invalid value for the **start** attribute, and **sort** and **lower** are invalid attributes for **<ol>**.

7. A - Objective 031.1

A version control system (VCS) is a software program that helps software developers manage changes to the source code. Using such a system, you can track every change to the source code, see who made a particular change, and, in case of a mistake, recover from a previous version. **Git**, **Subversion**, and **Mercurial** are three popular version control systems. Therefore, option A is the correct answer. For completeness, **Redis** is a common non-relational database, **NGINX** is an open-source software program mainly used for web servers and reverse proxies, and **SQL** is the most popular relational database language.

8. D - Objective 034.2

In JavaScript, the **let** statement is used to declare a block-scoped variable. Therefore, the variable **b**, which is declared inside curly brackets (it is assigned the value of **a**, hence **5**), is not accessible outside the block. As a result, an **Uncaught ReferenceError** message is given since **b** is not defined. This makes option D the correct answer. For completeness, remember that variables defined with **let** cannot be re-declared in the same block.

9. D - Objective 031.2

A relational database is a type of database based on the relational model of data. In short, data in relational databases is organized into tables that can be linked together based on common data (there is a relationship between records across multiple tables). Structured Query Language (SQL) is the language used for managing data in relational databases; that's why relational databases are also called SQL databases. The most popular relational databases are: **Microsoft SQL Server**, **SQLite**, **MySQL**, **MariaDB**, and **PostgreSQL**. A non-relational database, also called a NoSQL database, is a less structured type of database where the information to be stored is not sufficiently structured to be collected in tables and to define relationships between them. The storage model is optimized for the data to be stored, allowing for greater flexibility and adaptability. The most popular non-relational databases are: **MongoDB**, **Redis**, **Cassandra**, and **CouchDB**. Therefore, option D is the correct answer.

10. / - Objective 035.2

The **app** object conventionally specifies the Express application. In particular, the basic syntax **app.method(path, callback)** is used to specify a callback function (or handler function) that is called when the application receives a specific HTTP request to the path served by the route (**method** is the HTTP method of the request, such as GET, POST, or DELETE written in lowercase). Therefore, to complete the route, you need to specify the path served by the route and you can use **/** to indicate the site root (the base/root directory). For completeness, the route defined in the question returns the **Post Method OK** string whenever the application receives an HTTP POST request to the site root.

11. B - Objective 033.2

According to the explanation of question 5 of the Assessment Test, you can apply a style only to the first paragraph using an ID selector. Therefore, you must use the hash character followed by the **id** attribute of the paragraph you want to style (**#par_a**), making option B the correct answer. For completeness, the selector in option A is a class selector that applies to the first and third paragraphs, the selector in option C is a type selector that applies to all paragraphs, and the selectors in options D, E, and F are invalid selectors.

12. C - Objective 035.1

The **npm install** (or **npm i**) command is used to install all modules listed as **dependencies** and **devDependencies** in the **package.json** file. The command also creates a **node_modules** directory in the current project directory with the installed modules and generates a **package-lock.json** file describing the exact dependency tree. For this reason, dependencies are never bundled with the project itself. This makes option C the correct answer. To learn more about the **npm install** command, specifically how to use it to install a single module, take a look at answer 6 of the Assessment Test.

13. A - Objective 033.3

The **font-size** property is used to specify the size of a font. You can indicate the size in many ways including using absolute size values (based on the user's default font size) such as **small**, **medium**, **large**, **20px**, and **125%**, or using relative size values such as **larger** and

smaller to set the font larger or smaller than the font size of the parent element. Therefore, option A is the correct answer. For completeness, **bigger** is not a valid value for **font-size** and the **font-rsize** property does not exist.

14. B - Objective 033.4

In CSS, the **float** property is used to make an element float to the left, to the right, or not to make the element float. It removes the element from the normal flow of the document, while remaining part of the flow, and places it shifted to the left or right until it touches the edge of its container or another floating element. Other elements after a floating element flow around it; in this way a floating element goes above other block elements, but the text and inline elements within the container of the floating element wrap around the floating element itself. Therefore, option B is the correct answer. For completeness, the **flow**, **flow-control**, and **overlap** properties do not exist.

15. D - Objective 033.2

In CSS, to select an element with both the **a** and **b** classes, you can use the **.a.b** selector. Therefore, option D is the correct answer. For completeness, the selectors in options A, B, and C are not valid.

16. B - Objective 035.2

In Express, the built-in **express.static** middleware function is used to serve static files such as images and HTML, CSS, and JavaScript files. You just need to specify the name of the directory where your static resources are located and then load **express.static** with the **app.use()** method. Therefore, option B is the correct answer. For completeness, remember that you do not need to include the directory name in the URL to load a static file as Express looks for files relative to the directory itself.

Answers to Practice Exam 2

17. C - Objective 031.3

Hypertext Transfer Protocol Secure (HTTPS) is the secure version of the Hypertext Transfer Protocol (HTTP). It uses an encryption protocol to encrypt communications: Transport Layer Security (TLS), formerly known as Secure Sockets Layer (SSL). HTTPS version 1.1 uses TCP port 443 by default instead of TCP port 80 used by HTTP version 1.1. Therefore, option C is the correct answer. For completeness, the SMTP service is assigned to TCP port 25, the IMAP service is assigned to TCP port 143, and the FTP service is assigned to TCP port 21.

18. red - Objective 033.2

According to the explanation of question 12 of Practice Exam 1, the background color of the **<h1>** elements will be red. The property **background-color: red** is, in fact, marked as important (**!important**) and therefore takes precedence over **background-color: blue**.

19. D - Objective 035.2

Route parameters are named URL segments used to store values that are at specific locations in the URL. The name of each route parameter in the corresponding path is preceded by a colon and its value is stored in the **req.params** object (e.g. the path for a route with one route parameter is **'myPath/:firstParameter'**, while for a route with two route parameters is **'myPath/:firstParameter/:secondParameter'**). Therefore, the **id** parameter specified as a route parameter in the URL of an HTTP GET request can be accessed within the route handler function using **req.params.id**, making option D the correct answer.

20. A - Objective 032.4

In HTML, an **<input>** element is used to specify an interactive control for a user interface where a user can enter data. The different types of **<input>** elements that can be displayed depend on the specified **type** attribute and the **text** value in the question defines a single-line text field (this is the default value). To specify an initial value for this text field, you can use the **value** attribute, while to specify a short tip describing the expected value for this field, you can use the **placeholder** attribute (it can be seen as a sample value or an explanation of the field that is visible when the text field is empty and disappears when the user starts typing). Therefore, option A is the correct answer. For completeness, the **<input>** element does not have the **default**, **sample**, and **initia**l attributes.

21. B - Objective 032.4

In HTML, an **<input>** element of type **radio** is used to define a radio button. It is normally used in a radio group, which is a collection of radio buttons each of which describes an option. A radio group can be defined by assigning the same **name** attribute to each of the radio buttons belonging to the group. Once a radio group is created, if you select an entry in that group, the previously chosen entry (if any) for that group is automatically deselected so that only one entry within the group is selected at a time. This makes option B the correct answer. For completeness, the **<input>** element does not have the **group** attribute and **radio-group** is an invalid value for the **type** attribute.

22. B, C - Objective 034.3

In JavaScript, a function is created using the **function** keyword. You can create a function with a function declaration by specifying the function name and its parameters, but you can also use an alternative syntax that creates a function in a larger expression. In this case, a function is created with a function expression and can then be stored in a variable; as a result, the variable can be used to invoke the function. The difference between a function created with a function declaration and a function created with a function expression is that in the latter case the function name can be omitted, making that function anonymous. Functions created with a function declaration and functions created with a function expression are invoked in the same way;

however, functions created with a function declaration can be invoked before or after their initialization, while functions created with a function expression can be invoked only after their initialization. Therefore, options B and C are the correct answers. For completeness, **function myFunctionName(parameters) { //code to execute }** is an example of function created with a function declaration, while **const myVar = function(parameters) { //code to execute };** is an example of anonymous function created with a function expression.

23.2 - Objective 034.3

In JavaScript, the strict equality operator **===** returns **true** when both operands are of the same type and hold the same value. Unlike the **==** operator, if the operands are of different types, **===** does not attempt to convert them to the same data type to achieve a meaningful comparison. Therefore, the **if** statement returns **false** (variable **a** is assigned the string **100** and variable **b** the number **100**) and then variable **c** is assigned the number **2** which is logged in the browser console.

24.A - Objective 035.2

The **req.body** object contains key-value pairs of data submitted in the request body. To access a single field, you can use **req.body.fieldName**. This makes option A the correct answer. For completeness, remember that to properly read **req.body**, you must include a body parsing middleware such as **express.urlencoded()** to parse incoming requests with **urlencoded** payloads and **express.json()** to parse incoming requests with **JSON** payloads.

25.B - Objective 034.4

The DOM property named **classList** returns a live collection of the CSS class names of an element. This property is read-only, but you can use some methods to modify its associated CSS classes such as **add()** or

remove(), used to add or remove one or more classes respectively. Therefore, once you have selected all the **<h1>** elements of the document, you need to use a **for** loop to add the new class to each of the selected elements (at each iteration you need to use the **add()** method of the **classList** property for the selected element). The resulting **for** loop is **for (element of elements) { element.classList.add('main'); }** or alternatively **for (let i=0; i<elements.length; i++) { elements[i].classList.add('main'); }**. This makes option B the correct answer. For completeness, the **addClass()**, **classAdd()**, **addClassList()**, and **addToClassList()** methods do not exist.

26. C - Objective 033.1

The **<link>** tag is used to define the relationship between an external resource and an HTML page and should be placed in the **<head>** section of the page. In particular, you can use it to link an external style sheet to your current HTML page: the **href** attribute specifies where the external resource can be found and the **rel** attribute, which is required, specifies the relationship between the external resource and the HTML page (for an external style sheet the value is **stylesheet**). The **<link>** element is an empty element and does not have a closing tag. Therefore, option C is the correct answer. For completeness, the **<css>** tag does not exist.

27. C - Objective 034.4

The DOM method named **getElementById()** returns an element whose **id** matches the specified value or null if the element does not exist. Since the **id** should be unique for the specified element, you can use this method to access the corresponding HTML element very quickly. Therefore, once you have selected the element within the document by invoking **getElementById()** on the **document** object, you need to change its **innerHTML** property which specifies the inner HTML markup code of the selected element. This makes option C the correct answer. For completeness, **querySelectorById()** and **selectElementsById()** are not valid DOM methods.

28. A - Objective 035.3

The **db.run()** method is used to execute an SQL statement on a database (it does not retrieve any result data). In particular, to execute an **INSERT INTO** statement in your application code, you can use the following syntax: **db.run(sqlQuery, params, function(err){ //code in the callback function});**. This method executes the specified statement (**sqlQuery**) with the specified parameters (**params**) and then calls a callback function; if there are any errors, you can find detailed information about them in the **err** object. This makes option A the correct answer. For completeness, **db.execute()**, **db.insert()**, and **db.insertINTO()** are not valid methods.

29. D - Objective 032.3

A fragment is an internal page reference that is used to make the browser point to a specific spot on a web page. It is placed at the end of a URL and begins with a hash character (**#**) followed by the identifier of the resource it refers to. Therefore, to create a hyperlink pointing to the **<h3>** element with the **id** attribute set to **id_c** on the same page as the hyperlink, you need to specify the **#id_c** fragment in the **href** attribute of the **<a>** element. This makes option D the correct answer. For completeness, the **href** attribute specifies the link's destination, the **target** attribute specifies where to display the linked URL, and the **internal** attribute does not exist.

30. B - Objective 031.3

The **Accept** field in an HTTP request header is used to specify to the server which content types, expressed as MIME types, the client accepts for the response (in other words, the format of the requested resource). You can specify it using the **MIME_type/MIME_subtype** syntax to indicate a single MIME type and a single MIME subtype (e.g. **text/css** or **text/html**), the **MIME_type/*** syntax to indicate a single MIME type and any MIME subtype (e.g. **image/***), and the ***/*** syntax to indicate any MIME type and any MIME subtype (the ***** character means any value). Therefore, option B is the correct answer. For completeness, the **Expect** field is used to specify that a particular server behavior to properly handle the request is required by the client, and **Media-Type** and **Requested-Type** are invalid fields in an HTTP request header.

31.C - Objective 032.1

The **<meta>** element is used to specify the metadata of an HTML page. It must be placed in the **<head>** section and is a void (or empty or self-closing) element (it does not have a closing tag). The specific attributes for this element are: **name** which is used to provide a name for the metadata, that is, for the value in the **content** attribute (e.g. **author**, **description**, or **keywords**), **http-equiv** which is used to provide an HTTP header for the value in the **content** attribute (e.g. **content-type** or **refresh**), **content** which is used to provide the value for the **name** or **http-equiv** attribute, and **charset** which is used to provide the character encoding for the HTML document (e.g. **UTF-8**). Therefore, option C is the correct answer. For completeness, remember that **name** and **http-equiv** should be mutually exclusive and that **<meta>** also supports the core HTML attributes.

32.A - Objective 031.3

Status codes starting with 4 (4XX) are client error codes indicating that the request cannot be fulfilled due to an error from the client. In particular, the status code 403 means that the client does not have the rights to access the content and that its request has been rejected. The associated reason phrase is, in fact, **Forbidden**. This makes option A the correct answer. For completeness, 400 is the status code indicating that the server cannot process the request due to an apparent error on the client side such as malformed request syntax (its associated reason phrase is **Bad Syntax**), 408 is the status code indicating that the client request exceeded the time that the server was prepared to wait and the server decided to close the connection (its associated reason phrase is **Request Timeout**), and 500 is the status code indicating that the server encountered an unexpected situation that it does not know how to handle and which prevented it from fulfilling the request (its associated reason phrase is **Internal Server Error**). Finally, remember that in some cases servers can also send **404 Not Found** instead of **403 Forbidden** to hide the existence of a resource from a client that does not have the rights to access it (404 indicates that the server cannot find the requested target resource).

33. B, C, E - Objective 031.2

Back-end development refers to the build and maintenance of all server-side components that users do not interact with including servers, databases, scripting, application logic and integration, and APIs, involving all the behind-the-scenes activities that occur every time a user performs an action on a web site. Some programming languages for back-end development are: **PHP**, **Python**, **Ruby**, **Java**, **C#**, and **JavaScript** itself. Therefore, options B, C, and E are the correct answers. For completeness, as explained in answer 38 of Practice Exam 1, **HTML** and **CSS** are two languages for front-end development used respectively to define the structure and content of a web site and to apply styles to web pages.

34. D - Objective 034.3

The **for** statements allow you to create loops more compactly than **while** statements. In **for** loops, the initialization of the variable is performed before the start of the loop. Then the expression is evaluated and if the result is **true**, the code in the curly brackets is executed. Finally, the variable is iterated and the expression is evaluated again and so on, until a **false** value is returned; in that case the loop ends. The above can be summarized using the following pseudo-code: **for (VariableInitialization; expression; VariableIteration) { //This code is executed as long as the expression is true }**. Therefore, option D is the correct answer.

35. B, E - Objective 032.3

As explained in answer 3 of Practice Exam 1, the **target** attribute of the **<a>** element is used to specify where to display the URL set in the **href** attribute. Specifically, it can take the name of a browsing context (a tab, window, or **<iframe>**) or one of the following four keywords: **_self** (default value) which is used to display the linked URL in the current browsing context, **_blank** which is used to display the linked URL in a new window or tab depending on the web browser used and how it is configured, **_parent** which is used to display the linked URL in the parent browsing context if there's one or in the current browsing context if there is no parent, and **_top** which is used to display the linked URL in the topmost browsing context if there's one or in the current browsing context if there are no ancestors of the current browsing context. Therefore, options B and E are the correct answers.

36. C - Objective 035.3

In SQL, the **INSERT INTO** statement is used to insert a new record into a table. The correct syntax to use is: **INSERT INTO TableName (Column1, Column2, ... ColumnN) VALUES (Value1, Value2, ... ValueN)**, where **Column1, Column2, ... ColumnN** are the names of the columns in the table **TableName** where you want to insert the corresponding values **Value1, Value2, ... ValueN**. If you want to add values for all columns in the table, you don't need to specify the column names in the SQL statement; make sure, however, that the order of the values is the same as the columns in the table. Since column **name** is of type **VARCHAR(50)**, you need to specify the corresponding value in quotation marks, which is not to be done with column **code** of type **INTEGER**. Therefore, option C is the correct answer.

Answers to Practice Exam 2

37. C, E - Objective 033.4

In CSS, the **position** property is used to specify the type of positioning method for an HTML element. Possible values are: **static** (default value - the element is positioned according to the normal flow), **relative** (the element is positioned according to the normal flow and relative to its normal static position), **absolute** (the element is removed from the normal flow and is positioned relative to its closest positioned ancestor if present, otherwise it is positioned relative to the document body), **fixed** (the element is removed from the normal flow and is positioned relative to the viewport - it is not affected by scrolling), and **sticky** (the element is positioned according to the normal flow based on the user's scroll position - it is treated as a **relative** position until a specific offset position is reached in the viewport, from which point the element assumes a **fixed** position). The **top**, **right**, **bottom**, and **left** properties are used to determine the final position of elements whose **position** property is set to **relative**, **absolute**, **fixed**, or **sticky**. Elements whose **position** property is set to **static** are not affected by these four properties. Therefore, options C and E are the correct answers.

38. B - Objective 034.3

According to the explanation of question 22 of Practice Exam 2, option B correctly creates a function with a function expression and is therefore the correct answer. For completeness, the function simply concatenates two strings by placing a blank space between them. Finally, note that the function is anonymous and that it is stored in the **conc** variable (this way you can use **conc** to invoke the function).

39. A - Objective 035.3

When you successfully execute a **DELETE** statement with **db.run()**, the **this** object of the callback function contains the **changes** property which stores the number of database rows affected by the query (**this.changes**). Therefore, option A is the correct answer. For completeness, the **lines**, **rows**, and **numbers** properties do not exist for the **this** object. Finally, note that **this.changes** can also be very useful for **UPDATE** statements to find the numbers of updated rows.

40.B - Objective 034.2

According to the explanation of question 15 of Practice Exam 1, you can access the three properties of the **song** object using **song.title** (or **song["title"]** or **song['title']**), **song.singer** (or **song["singer"]** or **song['singer']**), and **song.year** (or **song["year"]** or **song['year']**). Therefore, option B is the correct answer.

Practice Exam 3

1. At the beginning of your JavaScript code, you define a constant using the **const max = 399;** instruction, but if some conditions are met, you must reassign it a value of **999**. Which of the following instructions can you use?

    A. const max = 999;

    B. max = 999;

    C. max = new Value(999);

    D. You cannot perform this operation

2. You are writing a CSS rule for all paragraphs that makes the text bold and extra-large using the **Helvetica** font or a generic **sans serif** font as a fallback if the browser doesn't support **Helvetica**. Which of the following CSS properties can you use in your rule?

    A. font-all: Helvetica, sans-serif x-large bold;

    B. font-*: Helvetica, sans-serif bold x-large;

    C. font-all: x-large; bold; Helvetica, sans-serif;

    D. font: bold x-large Helvetica, sans-serif;

    E. font: x-large; bold; Helvetica, sans-serif;

3. Which of the following is a valid route definition? Select two. Assume you have already loaded the **express** module and created an Express application named **app**.

   A. app.parse('/', function (req, res) {

   res.send('Successful response');

   })

   B. app.response('/sign', function (req, res) {

   res.send('Successful response');

   })

   C. app.get('/resource', function (req, res) {

   res.send('Successful response');

   })

   D. app.delete('/user', function (req, res) {

   res.send('Successful response');

   })

   E. app.update('/contact', function (req, res) {

   res.send('Successful response');

   })

4. You want to create a drop-down list with some options. Which of the following HTML elements can you use?

   A. You can use a **<dropdown>** element

   B. You can use an **<input>** element of type **dropdown**

   C. You can use an **<input>** element of type **select**

   D. You can use a **<select>** element

5. You want to run a Node.js application named **app.js**. Which of the following commands can you type in your terminal? Assume the file is in your current working directory (which is the project directory).

    A. node app.js

    B. js app.js

    C. nodejs app.js

    D. nexec ./app.js

6. Which of the following is not a primitive data type in JavaScript? Select two.

    A. string

    B. boolean

    C. float

    D. char

    E. undefined

7. The `<html>`, `<head>`, and `<body>` elements are used to structure an HTML document. Which of the following statements is true? Select two.

    A. `<html>` is a void element that must be placed before `<head>` and `<body>`

    B. The `<head>` section contains the document metadata that is not displayed in the web browser when the page is loaded

    C. `<head>` and `<body>` are void elements

    D. `<html>` is the first element in an HTML page and encloses only the `<title>` element

8. Given the following excerpt of JavaScript code:

```
var a = Number('');
console.log(a);
```

What is logged in the browser console?

A. 0

B. NaN

C. null

D. Uncaught ReferenceError: conversion between data types not allowed

9. You want to write a CSS rule that applies to all **<input>** elements of an HTML page and styles them when they get focus. Which of the following selectors can you use?

A. input:focus

B. onFocus.input

C. onFocusInput

D. input:onFocus

10. You want to have an **<input>** element of type **checkbox** pre-selected by default when the page loads. Which of the following attributes can you use?

A. selected

B. set

C. checked

D. validated

11. In the **<style>** element you can specify one or more CSS rules for your document. Which of the following is a valid CSS rule?

    A. p { font-size=10px }

    B. h1 { color: red; background-color: yellow }

    C. ul { font-size: large, color: blue }

    D. h2 { font-size=10px; background-color=purple }

    E. ol { color=blue, font-size=small }

12. Which of the following is a block-level element? Select two.

    A. <span>

    B. <ul>

    C. <div>

    D. <mark>

    E. <b>

13. Using Express, you want to access the **page** parameter specified in the query string of an HTTP GET request. Which of the following properties can you use within the route handler function? Assume that you have defined a **req** object representing the HTTP request and a **res** object representing the HTTP response.

    A. req.get.params.page

    B. req.param[0]

    C. req.query.page

    D. req.obj[0]

14. You have included an external JavaScript file within the **<script>** element in the **<head>** section of your HTML page. Which of the following statements is true?

    A. If you specify the **no-wait** attribute in the **<script>** tag, the script is downloaded in parallel with the parsing of the HTML page and when the download is complete, the script is executed; once the execution is finished, the HTML parsing is resumed

    B. If you specify the **wait** attribute in the **<script>** tag, the script is downloaded in parallel with the parsing of the HTML page, but its execution is deferred until the HTML parsing is complete.

    C. If you specify the **async** attribute in the **<script>** tag, the script is downloaded in parallel with the parsing of the HTML page and when the download is complete, the script is executed; once the execution is finished, the HTML parsing is resumed

    D. If you specify the **defer** attribute in the **<script>** tag, when the HTML parser processes the **<script>** tag, the script is downloaded and executed, blocking the rendering of the HTML page until these two operations are completed; only then the HTML parsing is resumed

15. What is the meaning of the 301 status code?

    A. Moved Permanently - The requested resource has been moved to a new permanent URL

    B. Found - The requested resource has been temporarily moved to a different URL

    C. Created - The request was successful and a new resource was created

    D. No Content - The request was successful and there is no content to send for this request

16. You want to load the static image files located in the folder named **images** in the same directory as the Node.js application using the **/img** virtual path prefix. Which of the following lines do you need to include in your application? Assume you have already loaded the **express** module and created an Express application named **app**.

    A. app.use(express.static('images', 'img'))

    B. app.use(express.static.prefix('/img', 'images'))

    C. app.use(express.prefix('/img'), express.static('images'))

    D. app.use('/img', express.static('images'))

17. Using Express, you want to query data from an SQLite table using a **SELECT** statement. Which of the following methods can you use? Assume that you have already loaded the **sqlite3** module and defined a constant named **db** to perform all database operations.

    A. db.query()

    B. db.select()

    C. db.all()

    D. db.retrieve()

18. Which of the following is an absolute URL to a file hosted on an external web site? Assume your domain name is **barfoo.foobar**.

    A. http://www.foo.bar/my_documents/foobar.pdf

    B. my_images/foo.jpg

    C. ../files/bar.zip

    D. /templates/barfoo.png

19. You want to write a **switch** statement that evaluates the value of the **distro** variable and writes, based on the match found, its corresponding distribution family in the browser console. Which of the following is a valid clause that you can use in your **switch**? Select two.

    A. eval('ubuntu'): console.log("Debian-based distro"); break;

    B. case "mint": console.log("Debian-based distro"); break;

    C. case "Rocky Linux" { console.log("Red Hat-based distro"); }

    D. eval('ClearOS') { console.log("Debian-based distro"); }

    E. case("Kubuntu"): case("Xubuntu"): case("Lubuntu"): console.log("Debian-based distro"); break;

    F. eval('Kubuntu' | 'Lubuntu' | 'Lubuntu') { console.log("Debian-based distro"); }

20. You want to disable an **<input>** element when a button is pressed. Which of the following **onClick** events can you use for your button? Assume that you can select the **<input>** element using **document.getElementById('input_id')**.

    A. onClick="document.getElementById('input_id').setAttribute('disabled', '');"

    B. onClick="document.getElementById('input_id').attributeList.disabled = true;"

    C. onClick="document.getElementById('input_id').set('disabled') = true;"

    D. onClick="document.getElementById('input_id').attributeList.set('disabled', '');"

Practice Exam 3

21. Using JavaScript, you want to sum the numbers in an array named **my_array**. Which of the following **for** loops can you use? Assume you have already defined a **sum** variable that has value 0 and an array of all numbers named **my_array**.

    A. for (let i = 0 ; i++ ; i < my_array.length) { sum = sum + my_array[i]; }

    B. for (let i = 0 ; i < my_array.length ; i++) { sum += array[i]; }

    C. for (let i = 0 ; i < my_array.length) { sum = sum + my_array[i]; i++; }

    D. for (let i = 0 ; i++; i < my_array.length) { sum + array[i]; }

    E. for (let i = 0 ; i < my_array.length ; i++) { sum = + array[i]; }

22. Which of the following statements about the programming process is true?

    A. Machine language is the set of statements and instructions written by a developer using a programming language that must be translated into source code in order to run

    B. In interpreted languages the interpreter reads the source code and creates a platform-specific executable file used for subsequent execution and whose extension depends on the interpreter used (for example **.js** for JavaScript or **.py** for Python)

    C. In compiled languages the source code is translated into machine language before program execution

    D. A program written in an interpreted language normally runs faster than a comparable program written in a compiled language

107

23. Which of the following statements about embedding audio and video files in an HTML document is true?

   A. You can embed audio and video files in an HTML document using the **<media>** element with the **type** attribute set to **audio** and **video** respectively

   B. You can embed audio and video files in an HTML document using the **<audio>** and **<video>** elements respectively

   C. You can embed audio and video files in an HTML document using the **<media>** element with the **src** attribute set to **audio** and **video** respectively

   D. You can embed audio and video files in an HTML document using the **<control>** element with the **source** attribute set to **audio** and **video** respectively

   E. You can embed audio and video files in an HTML document using the **<audio-src>** and **<video-src>** elements respectively

24. Which of the following statements about **em** and **rem** is true? Select two.

   A. If used on the **font-size** property of an element, **em** is relative to the **font-size** property of the direct or nearest parent of the element, while if used on other properties of the element, **em** is relative to the **font-size** property of the element itself

   B. **rem** is relative to the **<html>** font size

   C. **rem** is relative to the **<h1>** font size

   D. **em** is relative to the **font-size** property of the first element found in the HTML document

   E. **em** is relative to the **font-size** property of the **<h1>** element, if it exists; otherwise, a default value of **12px** is used

25. Which of the following is a valid CSS rule that specifies the position of a <div> element with the id attribute set to **id_div**?

    A. #id_div {

        position: relative 15px 50px;

        }

    B. #id_div {

        display: relative;

        offset-top: 15px;

        offeset-left: 50px;

        }

    C. #id_div {

        position: relative;

        top: 15px;

        left: 50px;

        }

    D. #id_div {

        display: 15px top 50px left relative;

        }

26. Which of the following SQL statements can you use to retrieve all columns of the table named **animals** for the category type **birds** only?

    A. SELECT * FROM birds IN animals;

    B. SELECT * FROM animals WHERE type='birds';

    C. SELECT birds FROM animals;

    D. SELECT * FROM animals WITH type='birds';

27. Using a JavaScript loop, you want to log each character of a specified string in the browser console. Which of the following instructions can you use? Assume that the string is assigned to a variable named **iterable**.

    A. for (const value of iterable) { console.log(value); }

    B. for (value in iterable.length) { console.log(value); }

    C. for (let i=0; i < iterable; i++) { console.log(i); }

    D. for (let i=0; i in iterable.length) { console.log(iterable[i]); }

28. Which of the following statements about **return** is true in JavaScript functions?

    A. There must be only one **return** statement

    B. There must be at least one **return** statement

    C. A function may not contain a **return** statement

    D. The **return** statement must be followed by an expression whose value is returned to the caller

29. Which of the following statements about REST is true?

    A. It is designed to be stateful and requires the server to keep track of session data during client/server communication

    B. It is based on the basic methods available in HTTP such as GET, POST, PUT, and DELETE

    C. It is not cacheable to improve performance

    D. It uses HTML as a standardized protocol to allow client/server communication

30. In HTTP version 1.1, which of the following fields in the HTTP request header specifies the host and port number of the server to which the resource is requested?

   A. DomainURL

   B. Host

   C. Hostname

   D. FQDN

31. Which of the following is a non-relational database? Select two.

   A. PostgreSQL

   B. MongoDB

   C. Redis

   D. MariaDB

   E. MySQL

32. Using Express and Embedded JavaScript, you want to send the client the response obtained by combining the **my_view** template and the **my_param** object. Which of the following methods can you use? Assume that **my_view** is in the **views** directory and that you have defined a **req** object representing the HTTP request and a **res** object representing the HTTP response.

   A. res.sendTemplate('my_view', my_param);

   B. res.sendTemplate([my_param], 'my_view');

   C. res.render(my_param: my_param, 'my_view');

   D. res.render('my_view', { my_param: my_param});

33. You have selected a **<div>** element using:

    ```
    const element = document.getElementById('div_b');
    ```

    Which of the following assignment statements can you use to select all **<p>** elements within the selected **<div>**?

    A. const elements = document.getElementsByTagName("p");

    B. const elements = document.querySelectorAll("p");

    C. const elements = element.getElementsByTagName("p");

    D. const elements = element.querySelectByTagName("p");

34. You have a **<div>** element with a fixed width of 500px. How can you center it horizontally?

    A. You can use the property **margin: 0 auto;**

    B. You can use the property **block-align: center;**

    C. You can use the property **text-align: center;**

    D. You can use the property **position: 0 auto;**

35. You want to place some content, indirectly related to the main content of the document, as a sidebar in your HTML page. Which of the following HTML elements can you use?

    A. <aside>

    B. <snav>

    C. <nav>

    D. <section>

    E. <sidebar>

36. Given the following HTML code:

```
<h1 id="h_a" class="cl_a"> A heading </h1>
<p id="par_a" class="cl_a"> A paragraph </p>
<ul class="cl_a">
  <li> First element </li>
  <li> Second element </li>
  <li> Third element </li>
  <li> Fourth element </li>
</ul>
```

Which of the following CSS rules can you use to make the text of all these elements x-small?

   A. #cl_a { font-size: x-small }

   B. p, #h_a { font-size: x-small }

   C. h_a, par_a, ul { font-size: x-small }

   D. .cl_a { font-size: x-small }

37. You want to write a CSS rule that sets the text to italics for all paragraphs in the **<div>** element with the **id** attribute set to **fdiv** and for all paragraphs in the **<div>** elements with the **class** attribute set to **fclass**. Which of the following rules can you use?

   A. #fdiv p, .fclass p { font-style: italic }

   B. #fdiv p, div.fclass p { font-style: italic }

   C. fdiv#p, fclass.p { font-style: italic }

   D. fdiv#p, fclass#p { font-style: italic }

38. You want to delete all rows in the table named **animals** with the category type **birds**. Which of the following SQL statements can you use? Assume that you are using SQLite as your database.

    A. DELETE type='birds' FROM animals;

    B. CANCEL FROM animals IF type='birds'

    C. CANCEL type FROM animals IF 'birds'

    D. DELETE FROM animals WHERE type='birds';

39. Which of the following is not an HTTP method? Select two.

    A. POST

    B. PUT

    C. UPDATE

    D. HEAD

    E. REPLACE

40. Which of the following is a valid **<meta>** element? Select two.

    A. <meta name="author"> myName mySurname </meta>

    B. <meta http-equiv="refresh" content="10; url=https://www.mySite.com">

    C. <meta name="keywords" content="myFirstKeyword, mySecondKeyword, myThirdKeyword">

    D. <meta name="charset"> UTF-8 </meta>

    E. <meta method="http-equiv" type="refresh" value="content="10; url=https://www.my_site.com">

Answers to Practice Exam 3

1. **D - Objective 034.2**

   The **const** keyword is used to define a constant, that is a read-only/constant reference to a value. Therefore, the constants thus defined cannot be re-declared and cannot be reassigned. This makes option D the correct answer. For completeness, remember that a constant has a block scope and if a constant is an object or an array, its items or properties can be updated or removed.

2. **D - Objective 033.3**

   To accomplish the task of the question, you need to set three individual font properties: **font-weight** which specifies the weight/boldness of a font (e.g. **normal**, **bold**, **lighter**, or **900**), **font-size** which specifies the size of a font (e.g. **small**, **large**, or **20px**), and **font-family** which specifies one or more specific or generic font family names separated by commas (e.g. **serif**, **Helvetica**, or **sans-serif**). Alternatively, you can use the **font** property which sets all the different properties of an element's font (**font** is a shorthand for **font-style font-variant font-weight font-size/line-height font-family** and the individual properties must be written in this particular order with a **/** between **font-size** and **line-height** and are not separated by semicolons). Therefore, in your CSS rule you can specify either the individual properties **font-weight: bold; font-size: x-large; font-family: Helvetica, sans-serif;** or the **font: bold x-large Helvetica, sans-**

serif; property, making option D the correct answer. For completeness, the **font-all** and **font-*** properties do not exist.

3. C, D - Objective 035.2

According to the explanation of question 10 of Practice Exam 2, options C and D contain a valid route definition and are therefore the correct answers. They return the **Successful response** string whenever the application receives an HTTP GET request to the **/resource** path and an HTTP DELETE request to the **/user** path, respectively. For completeness, the **app.parse()**, **app.response()**, and **app.update()** methods do not exist.

4. D - Objective 032.4

In HTML, the **<select>** element is used to create a drop-down list whose available options are specified by the **<option>** elements within the **<select>** element. To preselect a specific option when the page is loaded, you need to specify the **selected** attribute in the corresponding **<option>** element. If you have many options, it is a good practice to group related options within **<optgroup>** elements. Therefore, option D is the correct answer. For completeness, the **<input>** element does not have the **select** and **dropdown** types and **<dropdown>** is an invalid HTML element.

5. A - Objective 035.1

The usual way to run a Node.js application is to use the **node** command followed by the name of the file you want to run. Therefore, to run a Node.js application named **app.js** located in your current working directory, you need to use the **node app.js** command, making option A the correct answer. For completeness, remember that if the file is not in your current working directory, you need to specify the full path to the file.

6. C, D - Objective 034.2

In JavaScript, a primitive data type is any data with a primitive value, that is, a value that is not an object without properties and methods. Primitive values are immutable and cannot be changed. JavaScript has seven primitive data types: **string**, **number**, **bigint**, **boolean**, **undefined**, **symbol**, and **null**. Therefore, options C and D are the correct answers.

7. B - Objective 032.1

According to the explanation of question 5 of Practice Exam 1 and question 1 of Practice Exam 2, option B is the correct answer. Take a look at the answers to these questions to learn more about the **<html>**, **<head>**, **<body>**, and **<title>** elements.

8. A - Objective 034.2

In JavaScript, type conversion refers to the process of converting one data type into another. It is an explicit conversion that most of the time occurs using built-in functions such as **String()**, **Number()**, and **Boolean()**. Specifically, the **Number()** function is used to convert the value passed as an argument to a number; if it cannot be converted, **NaN** (**Not a Number**) is returned. Converting an empty string to a number returns **0**. This makes option A the correct answer.

9. A - Objective 033.2

In CSS, a pseudo-class is a keyword added to a selector that specifies a particular state of the selected elements. In particular, the **:focus** pseudo-class is used to indicate when an element has focus. Therefore, if you want to style all **<input>** elements of an HTML page when they get focus, you can use the **input:focus** selector. This makes option A the correct answer. For completeness, the **:onFocus** pseudo-class does not exist, while the **onFocus.input** and **onFocusInput** selectors are invalid. Finally, remember that an **<input>** element get focus when it is clicked, when the user tabs into it, or when the user clicks on the **<label>** element associated with the **<input>** field.

10. C - Objective 032.4

The **checked** attribute is a Boolean attribute that is used to specify whether a checkbox (an **<input>** element of type **checkbox**) is pre-selected by default when the page is loaded. Therefore, option C is the correct answer. For completeness, the **selected**, **set**, and **validated** attributes do not exist for the **<input>** element. Finally, remember that the **checked** attribute can also be used on a radio button (an **<input>** element of type **radio**) to specify whether it is the one currently selected in its radio group when the page is loaded.

11. B - Objective 033.1

A CSS rule has the following basic syntax: **CSS_Selector { property: value }**, where **CSS_Selector** is the pattern used to select the element or elements you want to style (for example, it allows you to match elements by type or class). If you want to change multiple properties, you need to separate them with a semicolon. Therefore, option B is the correct answer. For completeness, the rule **h1 { color: red; background-color: yellow }** sets the text color to red and the background color to yellow for all **<h1>** elements on the page.

12. B, C - Objective 032.2

HTML elements are generally classified into block-level elements and inline-level elements. Block-level elements start on a new line (browsers normally add a new line both before and after the element) and take up as much horizontal space as possible (all available width), while inline elements do not start on a new line and only take up as much width as necessary (the space required by the content). Examples of block-level elements are: **<p>**, **<h1>**, **<h2>**, **<h3>**, **<h4>**, **<h5>**, **<h6>**, **<ul>**, **<ol>**, **<li>**, **<div>**, **<main>**,

<header>, **<footer>**, and **<section>**. Examples of inline-level elements are: **<em>**, **<b>**, **<i>**, **<span>**, **<mark>**, **<a>**, and **<strong>**. Therefore, options B and C are the correct answers.

13. C - Objective 035.2

The query string is the part of a URL after the question mark (**?**) that is used to send small information to the server via the URL in the form of key-value pairs separated by an ampersand (**&**). Each query string parameter found in a URL is available in the **req.query** object. Therefore, the **page** parameter specified in the query string can be accessed within the route handler function using **req.query.page**. This makes option C the correct answer. For completeness, remember that **req.query** is primarily used for searching, sorting, filtering, and pagination.

14. C - Objective 034.1

The **<script>** tag has two Boolean attributes that can be useful for optimizing the loading time of a web page: **async** and **defer**. If you specify the **async** attribute, the script is downloaded in parallel with the parsing of the HTML page and when the download is complete, the script is executed, effectively blocking the rendering of the HTML page; once the execution is finished, the HTML parsing is resumed. On the other end, if you specify the **defer** attribute, the script is downloaded in parallel with the parsing of the HTML page, but its execution is deferred until the HTML parsing is complete. This makes option C the correct answer. For completeness, **wait** and **no-wait** are not valid attributes for the **<script>** tag. Finally, remember that if neither the **async** nor the **defer** attribute is specified, when the HTML parser processes the **<script>** tag, the script is downloaded and executed, blocking the rendering of the HTML page until these two operations are completed; only then the HTML parsing is resumed.

15.A - Objective 031.3

Status codes starting with 3 (3XX) are redirection codes indicating that the client may take additional action to complete the request. In particular, the status code 301 means that the requested resource has been moved to a new permanent URL which is provided in the response. The associated reason phrase is, in fact, **Moved Permanently**. Therefore, option A is the correct answer. For completeness, **Found** is the reason phrase for the status code 302 indicating that the requested resource has been temporarily moved to a different URL, **Created** is the reason phrase for the status code 201 indicating that the request was successful and a new resource was created, and **No Content** is the reason phrase for the 204 status code indicating that the request was successful and there is no content to send for this request.

16.D - Objective 035.2

A virtual path is a path that does not exist in the file system and is used to not show real folder names in the URL. To create a virtual path prefix for the files in a specified folder that are served by the **express.static** middleware, you just need to mount **express.static** at a specified mount path according to the following syntax: **app.use('MountPath', express.static('folder'))**. Therefore, option D is the correct answer.

17.C - Objective 035.3

The **db.all()** method is used to execute an SQL query with the specified parameters and invoke a callback function to access the rows in the result set. The syntax to use is: **db.all(sqlQuery, params, function(err, rows) { // code in the callback function });**. If the query is executed successfully, the **rows** object contains the result set of the query; if there are any errors, you can find detailed information about them in the **err** object. This makes option C the correct answer. For completeness, the **db.query()**, **db.select()**, and **db.retrieve()** methods do not exist.

18. A - Objective 032.3

An absolute URL is a URL that contains the entire address including the protocol, domain name, and path to a target resource. A relative URL is a URL that contains only the path to a target resource (no scheme or domain name is provided); in fact, it is assumed that the resource is on the same site as the web page and is part of the same domain. If the URL begins without a slash, it is relative to the current page, while if it begins with a slash, it is relative to the to the root (domain name) of the current web site. Therefore, assuming your domain name is **barfoo.foobar**, the URL in option A shows an absolute URL to a file that is hosted on an external website (**foo.bar**). This makes option A the correct answer. For completeness, **foo.jpg**, **bar.zip**, and **barfoo.png** are resources on the same site as your HTML document and are part of the **barfoo.foobar** domain.

19. B, E - Objective 034.3

The **switch** statement is used to evaluate an expression and execute the code associated with the **case** clause that matches the value of the expression (the code that is executed is the one that follows the colon until the **break** statement is reached). A **default** clause, if provided, is executed if the value of the expression doesn't match any other **case** clause. The last clause does not need a **break** statement and is usually the **default** clause. Several **case** clauses can also be grouped together if they share the same code to execute. Therefore, options B and E are the correct answers. For completeness, remember that **switch** uses a strict comparison to match the **case** clauses and the evaluated expression.

20. A - Objective 034.4

The DOM method named **setAttribute()** is used to set a value for an attribute on a specified element. The syntax to use is **setAttribute(name, value)** where **name** is a string representing the attribute name and **value** is a string representing the attribute value (any non-string **value** is automatically converted into a string). Therefore, once you have selected the **<input>** element with **document.getElementById('input_id')**, you can disable it by setting the **disabled** attribute to **true** with **setAttribute()**. Boolean attributes are considered **true** if they are present on the element; so you can just use the empty string as **value** or alternatively you can use the attribute name or any other string). This makes option A the correct answer. For completeness, the **attributeList** property does not exist and the **set** method is invalid.

21. B - Objective 034.3

According to the explanation of question 34 of Practice Exam 2, options B and E contain valid **for** loops: the first sums all the numbers in **my_array** (at each iteration the variable **sum**, which initially has the value 0, is incremented by the value present in **my_array** for that iteration), while the second assigns, at each iteration, the value present in **my_array** for that iteration to the variable **sum**. This makes option B the correct answer. For completeness, remember that **sum += array[i];** is equivalent to **sum = sum + my_array[i];**.

22. C - Objective 031.1

Source code is the set of statements and instructions written by a developer using a programming language. It must be translated into machine language in order to run. How this translation occurs depends on whether the programming language used is a compiled language or an interpreted language. A compiled language is a programming language in which the source code is translated into machine language before program execution. An interpreted language is a programming language in which the source code is translated into machine language at the same time the program runs; an interpreter reads the source code and executes its instructions and statements each time the program is run. A program written in an interpreted language normally runs slower than a comparable program written in a compiled language.

On the other hand, interpreted languages are normally platform independent (instead, a compiled program usually works only on the platform for which it was compiled). Examples of compiled programming languages are: **C**, **C++**, and **C#**. Examples of interpreted programming languages are: **JavaScript**, **Python**, and **PHP**. Therefore, option C is the correct answer.

23. B - Objective 032.3

In HTML, the **<audio>** element is used to embed sound content in an HTML document, while the **<video>** element is used to embed a media player that supports video playback. For both elements, the **src** attribute can be used to specify the location of the source. Alternatively, you can specify one or more sources using the **<source>** element and the browser will choose the first one it supports. This makes option B the correct answer. For completeness, the **<media>**, **<control>**, **<audio-src>**, and **<video-src>** elements do not exist. Finally, remember that the closing tags for **<audio>** and **<video>** are **</audio>** and **</video>** and that the content inside the opening and closing tags is displayed only in browsers that do not support the **<audio>** and **<video>** elements.

24. A, B - Objective 033.3

In CSS, **rem** and **em** are two relative units. In particular, **rem** is relative to the font size of the root element (hence the **<html>** element), while **em** is relative to the **font-size** property of the direct or nearest parent of the element when used on the **font-size** property of an element, and is relative to the **font-size** property of the element itself when used on the other properties of the element. Therefore, options A and B are the correct answers. For completeness, remember that relative units are scalable and can be very useful in responsive design.

25. C - Objective 033.4

According to the explanation of answer 37 of Practice Exam 2, option C specifies the right CSS rule to use and is therefore the correct answer. This rule, in fact, specifies that the positioning method for the **<div>** element is **relative** and the **top** and **left** properties determine the final position of the element in relation to its normal static position. For completeness, the **display** property is used to specify how an element is displayed, while the **offset-top** and **offset-left** properties do not exist.

26. B - Objective 035.3

According to the explanation of question 10 of the Assessment Test and question 32 of Practice Exam 1, option B contains a valid SQL statement that you can use to accomplish the task of the question and is therefore the correct answer.

27. A - Objective 034.3

In JavaScript, the **for...of** statement is used to create a loop that iterates through the values of an iterable object such as a string or array. For strings, at each iteration each distinct character within the string is assigned to the specified variable starting with the first character and the code in the curly brackets is executed. Therefore, option A is the correct answer. For completeness, **for (const value of iterable) { console.log(value); }** is equivalent to **for (let i=0; i < iterable.length; i++) { console.log(iterable[i]); }**.

28. C - Objective 034.3

In a JavaScript function, the **return** statement is used to stop the execution of the function and return a value to the caller. It is usually followed by an expression whose value is returned to the caller and if the expression is omitted, **undefined** is returned instead. A function can contain multiple **return** statements, but it can also contain none at all; if there is no **return** statement, the function returns **undefined**. Therefore, option C is the correct answer.

29.B - Objective 031.2

REST is an acronym for REpresentational State Transfer and is an architectural style for providing a communication set of rules between systems on the web. REST services are based on a client/server architecture: a client requests a specific resource and the server sends back the current state of the resource in a standardized representation. There is therefore a separation between the client and server components that can evolve independently. The REST architecture provides a uniform interface to allow client/server communication using a specific language recognized by both components. HTTP is typically the standardized protocol used in REST services; REST uses, in fact, the basic HTTP methods such as GET, POST, PUT, and DELETE. REST is designed to be stateless: there is no session state and a client and a server always include in their communication the necessary information needed to perform the request (each interaction is independent - for example the client must authenticate itself every time it makes a request). REST is also cacheable (all resources can be cached to improve performance) and allows for an architecture with multiple layers of servers, each of which has specific functions (additional layers do not affect the client/server communication). Based on the above, option B is the correct answer. For completeness, remember that in a REST architecture a server can also add functionality to the client by sending it executable code such as Java applets and client-side scripts such as JavaScript (this is an optional feature named Code on Demand).

30.B - Objective 031.3

The **Host** field in an HTTP request header is used to specify the host and port number of the server to which the resource is requested. If no port is included, the default port for the requested service is assumed.

In a typical scenario, an HTTP server hosts many web sites: the server will be then able to identify which site the request is for via the **Host** field (each host is a virtual host). Therefore, option B is the correct answer. For completeness, **DomainURL**, **Hostname**, and **FQDN** are invalid fields.

31. B, C - Objective 031.2

According to the explanation of question 9 of Practice Exam 2, **MongoDB** and **Redis** are two popular non-relational databases. This makes options B and C the correct answers.

32. D - Objective 035.2

The **res.render()** method is used to render a template file and send the rendered HTML data to the client. The correct syntax to use is **res.render(view [, locals] [, callback])** where **view** is the template file, **locals** is an object containing local variables for the template, and **callback** is a callback function name (**locals** and **callback** are optional). This makes option D the correct answer. For completeness, the **sendTemplate()** method does not exist. Finally, note that the template file extension **.ejs** is not provided as Express resolves it automatically (EJS is set as the view engine for the Express application and **views** is by default the folder in the application root directory where the template files are located).

33. C - Objective 034.4

The DOM method named **getElementsByTagName()** returns a collection of elements with the tag name specified in round brackets. It can be called on the **document** object to search the complete document or on a specific element to search only for elements that are descendants of the specified element. Therefore, to select all <p> elements within the selected <div> element and assign them to the constant **elements**, you can use **const elements =**

element.getElementsByTagName("p"); (note that the specified **<div>** is assigned to the constant **element**). This makes option C the correct answer. For completeness, **document.querySelectorAll("p")** and **document.getElementsByTagName("p")** can be used to select all **<p>** elements in the web page and **querySelectByTagName()** is an invalid method. Finally, remember that **getElementsByTagName()** returns a live collection of elements (an array-like object) that is automatically updated when the underlying document is changed: so be careful when iterating over the returned elements (if you want a static list, you can use **querySelectorAll()** instead).

34.A - Objective 033.4

In CSS, the **margin** property is used to set a margin on all four sides of an element. When one value is specified, it refers to all four sides. When two values are specified, the first refers to the top and bottom and the second to the left and right. When three values are specified, the first refers to the top, the second to the left and right, and the third to the bottom. When four values are specified, they refer to the top, right, bottom, and left (clockwise). A value can be specified as length, percentage, or with the keyword **auto**. In particular, you can use this last value to center an element horizontally by setting the property **margin: 0 auto;** (the first value indicates that the top and bottom margins are both set to 0, while the second value indicates that the browser automatically determines the left and right margins, which are then set to the same size). This makes option A the correct answer. For completeness, the **position** property is used to specify the type of positioning method for an HTML element, the **text-align** property is used to specify the horizontal alignment of text within an HTML element, and the **block-align** property does not exist. Finally, remember that the **margin** property is a shorthand for **margin-top**, **margin-right**, **margin-bottom**, and **margin-left** (so **margin: 0 auto;** can be rewritten as **margin-top: 0; margin-right: auto; margin-bottom: 0; margin-left: auto;**).

35.A - Objective 032.2

The **<aside>** element is used to define some content indirectly related to the main content of the document. It is often used for sidebars to display secondary information. This makes option A the correct answer. For completeness, the **<nav>** element is used to provide navigation links within the current document or to other documents, the **<section>** element is used to define a single section of the HTML document (it is not a standalone content and is related to its surrounding semantic element such as the main content), and the **<snav>** and **<sidebar>** elements do not exist.

36.D - Objective 033.2

According to the explanation of question 5 of the Assessment Test, you can apply a style to all elements using a class selector (note that all elements have the same **class** attribute). Therefore, you must then use the period (**.**) followed by the class name of the elements you want to style (**cl_a**). This makes option D the correct answer. For completeness, option A specifies an ID selector that has no match (no element has an **id** attribute set to **cl_a**), option B specifies two selectors that make the text x-small only for the heading and paragraph (**p** is a type selector that applies to the paragraph and **#h_a** is an ID selector that applies to the heading), and option C specifies only one valid selector that makes the text x-small for the unordered list (**h_a** and **par_a** are invalid selectors, while **ul** is a type selector that applies to the unordered list).

37.B - Objective 033.2

In CSS, a descendant selector is used to match all descendant elements of a specified element. A first selector, called ancestor, is then followed by a second selector, called descendant, separated by a space. Therefore, to select all paragraphs in the **<div>** element with the **id** attribute set to **fdiv**, you can use the **#fdiv p** selector (**#fdiv** is the ancestor and **p** is the descendant). Instead, to select all paragraphs in the **<div>** elements with the **class** attribute set to **fclass**, you can use the **div.fclass p** selector (**div.fclass** is the ancestor and **p** is the descendant). To group these two selectors, you can separate them with a comma, making option B the correct answer. For completeness, the **.fclass p** selector is used to match all paragraphs in all elements (not just **<div>**) with the **class** attribute set to **fclass**, while the **fdiv#p**, **fclass.p**, and **fclass#p** selectors are invalid.

38. D - Objective 035.3

In SQL, the **DELETE** statement is used to delete one or more existing records in a specified table. The syntax to use is: **DELETE FROM TableName WHERE search_condition;**. The **WHERE** clause is optional and indicates the rows of the table **TableName** to be deleted. If you omit the **WHERE** clause, all rows in the table will be removed. Therefore, option D is the correct answer. For completeness, the **CANCEL** statement does not exist.

39. C, E - Objective 031.3

An HTTP method specifies the action the client wants to perform on a resource at a given URI (Uniform Resource Identifier). Common HTTP methods are: GET which is used to request data from the server, HEAD which is used to request HTTP headers from the server, for example to get additional information about a large resource before downloading it (no content of the requested resource is sent by the server), POST which is used to send data to the server to create or update a resource (it is usually used to add a resource, for example when submitting an HTML form or when uploading data to the server), PUT which is used to create a new resource or replace/update an existing one on the server (it is usually used to update data to the server), and DELETE which is used to delete a resource from the server. Instead, UPDATE and REPLACE are not valid HTTP methods. Therefore, options C and E are the correct answers. For completeness, remember that GET, HEAD,

PUT, and DELETE are defined as idempotent, i.e. multiple identical requests have the same effect as a single request.

40. B, C - Objective 032.1

According to the explanation of question 31 of Practice Exam 2, options B and C contain two valid **<meta>** elements and are therefore the correct answers. Specifically, the **<meta>** element in option B redirects a web page to **https://www.mySite.com** after 10 seconds, while the **<meta>** element in option C specifies a series of keywords (**myFirstKeyword**, **mySecondKeyword**, and **myThirdKeyword**) related to the HTML page that are useful for SEO. For completeness, the **method**, **type**, and **value** attributes are invalid for **<meta>**.

Practice Exam 4

1. Using Embedded JavaScript (EJS), within which of the following tags in a template file can you insert flow control structures such as JavaScript **if** and **for** statements?

    A. Between the <%! and !%> tags

    B. Between the <%# and %> tags

    C. Between the <% and %> tags

    D. Between the <$ and $> tags

2. You want to hide the <div> element with the **id** attribute set to **div_a** by setting its inline CSS **display** property directly in the JavaScript code. Which of the following instructions can you use? Assume that you are using JavaScript to access the Document Object Model (DOM) elements.

    A. document.querySelector("div_a").display = "none";

    B. document.selectById("div_a").style.display = "none";

    C. document.querySelector("#div_a").style.display = "none";

    D. document.selectById("#div_a").display = "none";

    E. document.selectById("#div_a").style.display = "none";

3. Given the following excerpt of JavaScript code:

```
let x = 5;
let y = 15;
console.log("The result is " + x + y);
```

What is logged in the browser console? Write the entire logged string.

4. Which of the following block elements can you use to describe the semantic structure of an HTML page? Select two.

   A. `<h0>`

   B. `<footnote>`

   C. `<heading>`

   D. `<main>`

   E. `<footer>`

5. You want to specify the style for some elements of a single HTML page, thus defining multiple CSS rules for that page. Which of the following statements is true? Suppose you do not want to link external style sheets to your HTML page.

   A. You can write your CSS rules in the **<head>** section of your HTML page within a **<link>** element

   B. You can write your CSS rules in the **<head>** section of your HTML page within a **<style>** element

   C. You can write your CSS rules outside the **<html>** element within a section starting with **CSS** and ending with **END CSS**

   D. You can write your CSS rules outside the **<html>** element, within a **<style>** element

6. Which of the following is not a valid attribute that you can specify for the **<meta>** element? Select three.

   A. content

   B. http-method

   C. keyword

   D. http-equiv

   E. page-description

7. Which of the following is a valid comment line in HTML?

   A. // This is a comment

   B. <!-- This is a comment -->

   C. <# This is a comment #>

   D. #<# This is a comment #>#

   E. % This is a comment %

8. Which of the following statements about a primary key in a relational database table is true?

   A. A primary key is always made up of only one column

   B. A primary key can have **NULL** values

   C. A primary key is used to identify a table in a relational database and can be used in SQL queries in the **FROM** clause in place of the table name

   D. A primary key must have a unique value for each record in a table

9. The **margin** property is used to create extra space around an element. What other CSS property can you use to create extra space within an element instead?

    A. internal-margin

    B. filling

    C. internal-spacing

    D. padding

10. Given the following CSS rules:

```
li {
  background-color: green
}
li {
  background-color: purple
}
```

What will the background color of the `<li>` elements be? Just write the color name in lowercase. Assume that only these two CSS rules apply to your HTML page.

11. Consider the following selector: **.abc .xyz** (note the space). Which of the following statements about this selector is true?

    A. It is used to select all elements with both **abc** and **xyz** classes

    B. It is used to select all elements with class **abc** that are descendants of elements with class **xyz**

    C. It is used to select all elements with class **xyz** that are descendants of elements with class **abc**

    D. It is an invalid selector

12. Given the following opening tag of a **<form>** element in an HTML page:

```
<form action="/send_data" method="post">
```

Which of the following Express routes processes the data when submitting the form? Assume you have already loaded the **express** module and created an Express application named **app**.

    A. app.get('/send_data', function (req, res) {

        res.send("Received data");

    })

    B. app.post('/send_data', function (req, res) {

        res.send("Received data");

    })

    C. app.send_data('post', function (req, res) {

        res.send("Received data");

    })

    D. app.send_data('get', function (req, res) {

        res.send("Received data");

    })

13. Which of the following is not a web browser?

    A. Firefox

    B. Mercurial

    C. Safari

    D. Edge

14. Which of the following is not an interpreted programming language?

    A. JavaScript

    B. PHP

    C. C++

    D. Python

15. Which of the following is a valid route definition with two route parameters? Assume you have already loaded the **express** module and created an Express application named **app**.

    A. app.get('/user/%name%/%surname%', function (req, res) {
        res.send(req.params.name + " " + req.params.surname);
    })

    B. app.get('/user', $name, $surname, function (req, res) {
        res.send(req.params.name + " " + req.params.surname);
    })

    C. app.get('/user/$name/$surname', function (req, res) {
        res.send(req.params.name + " " + req.params.surname);
    })

    D. app.get('/user', ':name:surname', function (req, res) {
        res.send(req.params.name + " " + req.params.surname);
    })

    E. app.get('/user/:name/:surname', function (req, res) {
        res.send(req.params.name + " " + req.params.surname);
    })

16. Using **npm**, you want to initialize a new Node.js project. Which of the following commands can you use? Assume you don't have any initialization packages.

    A. npm json

    B. npm new package.json

    C. npm build package.json

    D. npm init

17. You want to write a CSS rule that sets the background color of a paragraph in an HTML page to yellow when the mouse is over it. Which of the following rules can you use?

    A. over.p { background-color: yellow }

    B. p:onMouseOver { background-color: yellow }

    C. p:hover { background-color: yellow }

    D. onMouseOver.p { background-color: yellow }

    E. onHover.p { background-color: yellow }

18. You want to write **Hello World** in bold within your paragraph, while also adding semantic importance. Which of the following elements can you use?

    A. <b> Hello World </b>

    B. <bold> Hello World </bold>

    C. <strong> Hello World </strong>

    D. <mark> Hello World </mark>

19. You want to force an **<h2>** element to move below any floating element that precedes it. Which of the following properties can you use in the CSS rule for that **<h2>** element?

    A. br-float: any;

    B. cr-float: right left;

    C. clear: both;

    D. skip: all;

20. You want to write a **switch** statement that evaluates the value of the variable named **type** and takes some action based on the match found. Which of the following is a valid clause that you can set to perform a default action when no other matches occur?

    A. case default { console.log("Invalid type"); break; }

    B. default case: console.log("Invalid type"); break;

    C. default: console.log("Invalid type"); break;

    D. case(default) { console.log("Invalid type"); break; }

21. Using Embedded JavaScript (EJS), you want to change the default folder where template files are located so that they can be stored in the **custom** folder in the application root directory. Which of the following instructions can you use? Assume you have already loaded the **express** module and created an Express application named **app**.

    A. app.use('custom', 'default-folder')

    B. app.set('views', 'custom')

    C. app.set('default', 'custom', 'views')

    D. app.use('views', 'ejs-default', 'custom')

22. You want to define a **<form>** element that, upon submission, sends the form data to a file named **script_process.php** using POST. Which of the following is the correct opening tag of the **<form>** element you need to use? Assume that **script_process.php** is in the same location as the page containing the form.

    A. <form action="script_process.php" method="post">

    B. <form submit="script_process.php" http="post">

    C. <form submit="script_process.php" method="post">

    D. <form script="script_process.php" type="post">

23. You want to run an SQL **UPDATE** statement with **db.run()** by passing two parameters directly as method arguments. Which of the following characters do you need to use as a placeholder for those parameters within the SQL statement to be executed?

    A. !

    B. %

    C. ?

    D. #

24. Which of the following is a primitive data type in JavaScript?

    A. int

    B. number

    C. double

    D. decimal

25. You want to embed an image named **bar.jpg** which is in the folder one level up from the current folder where the HTML page is located. Which of the following values should be specified in the **src** attribute of the **<img>** element?

    A. bar.jpg

    B. img/bar.jpg

    C. ../bar.jpg

    D. ../../bar.jpg

26. You want to create a hyperlink that opens in users' e-mail application so that they can send an e-mail message to **foo@bar.com**. Which of the following values should be specified in the **href** attribute of the **<a>** element?

    A. sendmail: foo@bar.com

    B. mailto:foo@bar.com

    C. toaddress: foo@bar.com

    D. a:foo@bar.com

27. A web browser sends an HTTP GET request to a web server for a specified resource and the server successfully transmits it to the client. What will be the status code and its associate reason phrase in the HTTP response header?

    A. 200 OK

    B. 100 Success

    C. 001 Success

    D. A00 OK

28. You noticed that the **start** attribute of an ordered list is set to **10** and you want to remove it so that the list starts at **1**. Which of the following instructions can you use? Assume that you are using JavaScript to access the Document Object Model (DOM) elements and that you can select the list using **document.getElementById('list_id')**.

    A. document.getElementById('list_id').deleteAttribute('start');

    B. document.getElementById('list_id').removeAttribute('start');

    C. document.getElementById('list_id').start.remove();

    D. document.getElementById('list_id').start.delete();

29. Using JavaScript, you want to terminate the execution of statements in the current iteration of a loop if a particular condition is met and then continue with the next iteration. Which of the following instructions can you use?

    A. continue;

    B. next;

    C. break;

    D. jump;

30. You are writing a CSS rule that displays a blank line through the text for all elements that match a specified selector. Which of the following CSS properties can you use in your rule?

    A. text-special: through #000000;

    B. text-special: through #FFFFFF;

    C. text-decoration: line-through #000000;

    D. text-decoration: line-through #FFFFFF;

31. In HTTP version 1.1, which of the following fields in the HTTP response header is used to specify an identifier for a particular version of a requested resource?

   A. CID

   B. Content-Version

   C. Etag

   D. Version-ID

32. Browsing the Internet, a user types the following URL: **http://www.mysite.com:8080/test/user.html?f1=foo&f2=bar**. Which of the following statements is true?

   A. The requested resource is **/test/user.html?f1=foo&f2=bar**

   B. The requested resource is **/test/user.html**

   C. The requested resource is **f1=foo&f2=bar**

   D. The URL is invalid: the correct URL should be **http://www.mysite.com/test/user.html:8080?f1=foo&f2=bar**

33. Which of the following is a valid type that you can specify for an **<input>** element? Select three.

   A. date

   B. select

   C. hidden

   D. reset

   E. form-submit

34. Given the following excerpt of JavaScript code:

```
var array = [ 2, 5, 3, 7, 9, 11 ];
array.push(16);
array.pop();
console.log(array[5]);
```

What is the value logged in the browser console?

   A. 11

   B. 16

   C. 9

   D. 2

   E. 5

   F. 3

35. You want to include an external JavaScript file named **myJsCode.js** in the **<head>** section of your HTML page. Which of the following elements can you use?

   A. <script src="myJsCode.js"> </script>

   B. <link src="myJsCode.js" code="application/Javascript">

   C. <javascript src="myJsCode.js"> My JavaScript code </javascript>

   D. <ext src="myJsCode.js" type="application/javascript">

   E. <code-js src="myJsCode.js" embedded> My JavaScript code </code-js>

36. You want to set a double blue border for all elements that match a specified selector. Which of the following CSS properties can you use in your rule?

    A. border-style: double blue;

    B. set-border: double blue;

    C. border-line: double; border-color: blue;

    D. border: double blue;

37. What is the meaning of the following excerpt of JavaScript code?

    ```
    if(a == null) {
        console.log("Error - value not allowed");
    } else {
        console.log("Success - value allowed");
    }
    ```

    A. The code checks if the variable **a** is **undefined** or **null** and if so, writes an error message to the browser console; otherwise it writes a success message

    B. The code checks if the variable **a** is **undefined** and if so, writes an error message to the browser console; otherwise it writes a success message

    C. The code checks if the variable **a** is **null** and if so, writes an error message to the browser console; otherwise it writes a success message

    D. The code checks if the variable **a** is an empty string and if so, writes an error message to the browser console; otherwise it writes a success message

38. Which of the following statements about the **db.all()** and **db.each()** methods is true? Assume that you have already loaded the **sqlite3** module and defined a constant named **db** to perform all database operations.

    A. The **db.each()** method calls a callback function with an array containing all the results returned by the query, while the **db.all()** method calls a callback function for each row in the result set

    B. The **db.each()** method calls a callback function for each row in the result set, while the **db.all()** method calls a callback function with an array containing all the results returned by the query

    C. The **db.each()** method returns the first row matching the query, while the **db.all()** method returns all rows matching the query

    D. The **db.each()** method returns all rows matching the query, while the **db.all()** method returns the first row matching the query

39. Which of the following is a valid function created with a function declaration?

    A. logmsg typeof(function) { var d = new Date(); console.log("Message logged at",d); };

    B. function logmsg (var d = new Date(); console.log("Message logged at",d););

    C. function logmsg() { var d = new Date(); console.log("Message logged at",d); };

    D. logmsg function() { var d = new Date(); console.log("Message logged at",d); };

40. Which of the following statements about a web application is true?

    A. A web application must be installed on the computer before it can run

    B. A web application depends on the operating system you want to use it on

    C. A web application is typically tied to only one type of browser for which it was designed

    D. A web application uses the client/server model

Answers to Practice Exam 4

1. **C - Objective 035.2**

   In EJS, flow control structures can be inserted into a template file between the **<%** and **%>** tags: **<%** is the scriptlet tag used to specify the so-called logic and does not generate output, while **%>** is the plain ending tag and it is needed to close all the tags. Therefore, option C is the correct answer. For completeness, comments can be inserted within the **<%#** and **%>** tags and are not visible to the client.

2. **C - Objective 034.4**

   As described in answer 4 of Practice Exam 1, the DOM method named **querySelector()** returns the first element that matches the specified CSS selector or null if no match is found. Therefore, to select the **<div>** element with the **id** attribute set to **div_a**, you can use **document.querySelector("#div_a")**. Once selected, you can hide it by setting its inline **display** property to **none**: to do this, you need to use the read-only DOM property named **style** which returns the values of the **style** attribute for the selected element, that is a list of all inline styles properties. This makes option C the correct answer. For completeness, the **selectById()** method does not exist. Finally, remember that you need to use **#** in your CSS selector to select an element with a specific **id** and that if a CSS property contains a hyphen (-), you need to use the array-like notation (**[]**) to access the property (hence **style['CSSproperty']** instead of **style.CSSproperty**).

3. The result is 515 - Objective 034.2

In JavaScript, type coercion refers to the automatic/implicit conversion of values from one data type to another. Specifically, if one of the operands of the **+** operator is a string and the other operand is a non-string value, the non-string value is always implicitly coerced into a string. Therefore, the string logged in the browser console is: **The result is 515**.

4. D, E - Objective 032.2

To describe the semantic structure of an HTML page, you can use several block elements such as **<main>** which specifies the main content related to the central topic of a web page (there must be only one **<main>** element and its content must not be repeated across multiple web pages), **<header>** which defines a header for a web page or section (for a web page it usually contains a banner with a logo), and **<footer>** which defines a footer for a web page or section (for a web page it usually contains copyright and authorship information, contact information, and links to related documents). Therefore, options D and E are the correct answers. For completeness, **<h0>**, **<footnote>**, and **<heading>** are not valid HTML elements. Finally, remember that the **<aside>**, **<nav>**, and **<section>** elements described in answer 35 of Practice Exam 3 are also common block elements that you can use to describe the semantic structure of an HTML page.

5. B - Objective 033.1

If you want to style a single HTML page, you can write your CSS rules in the **<head>** section of the page you want to style within a **<style>** element. You can use the **type** attribute to specify the media type (known as the MIME type) of the **<style>** tag, which by default is **text/css**. Therefore, option B is the correct answer. For completeness, remember that if you want to link an external style sheet to your HTML document, you need to use the **<link>** tag.

Answers to Practice Exam 4

6. B, C, E - Objective 032.1

According to the explanation of question 31 of Practice Exam 2, **content** and **http-equiv** are two valid attributes that you can specify for the **<meta>** element. Therefore, options B, C, and E are the correct answers.

7. B - Objective 032.1

In HTML, a single-line or multiline comment is placed between the **<!--** and **-->** tags, and the text between these two tags is not displayed by web browsers. Comments are usually inserted to explain the source code so that it is more understandable by others. Therefore, option B is the correct answer. For completeness, note that two forward slashes (**//**) are used to introduce single-line comments in JavaScript.

8. D - Objective 035.3

In a relational database, a primary key is used to uniquely identify a record/row in a database table. A table can have only one primary key consisting of one or more columns. A primary key must have a unique value for each record in a table and cannot contain **NULL** values; it is usually used to implement relationships between tables and can also be generated automatically when a new record is inserted. Therefore, option D is the correct answer.

9. D - Objective 033.4

In CSS, the **padding** property is used to create an extra space for all four sides of an element (between the content and its borders). When one value is specified, it refers to all four sides. When two values are specified, the first refers to the top and bottom and the second to the left and right. When three values are specified, the first refers to the top, the second to the left and right, and the third to the bottom. When four values are specified, they refer to the top, right, bottom, and left (clockwise). A value can be specified as a length or a percentage.

Therefore, option D is the correct answer. For completeness, the **internal-margin**, **internal-spacing**, and **filling** properties do not exist. Finally, remember that **padding** is a shorthand for **padding-top**, **padding-right**, **padding-bottom**, and **padding-left**.

10. purple - Objective 033.2

According to the explanation of question 12 of Practice Exam 1, the background color of the **<li>** elements will be purple: in fact, if an element matches two or more equally specific rules, the last rule is applied to that element.

11. C – Objective 033.2

According to the explanation of question 37 of Practice Exam 3, **.abc .xyz** is a selector used to match all elements with class **xyz** that are descendants of elements with class **abc** (**.abc** is the ancestor, while **.xyz** is the descendant). Therefore, option C is the correct answer. For completeness, to select all elements with both **abc** and **xyz** classes, you need to use the **.abc.xyz** selector, while to select all elements with class **abc** that are descendants of elements with class **xyz**, you need to use the **.xyz .abc** selector.

12. B - Objective 035.2

The **<form>** tag in the question specifies that the HTTP method used to submit the form data is POST and that the URL that processes the data when submitting the form is **/send_data**. Therefore, according to the explanation of question 10 of Practice Exam 2, you need to specify **post** as the HTTP method served by the route and **/send_data** as the path served by the route. This makes option B the correct answer. For completeness, the route only sends back the **Received data** message to the client.

13.B − Objective 031.2

A web browser is an application program that allows people to access the World Wide Web. The most popular web browsers are: **Google Chrome**, **Safari**, **Microsoft Edge**, and **Mozilla Firefox**. Therefore, option B is the correct answer. For completeness, **Mercurial** is a version control system for software developers.

14.C − Objective 031.1

According to the explanation of question 22 of Practice Exam 3, **C++** is a compiled programming language, while **JavaScript**, **PHP**, and **Python** are interpreted programming languages. Therefore, option C is the correct answer.

15.E - Objective 035.2

According to the explanation of question 19 of Practice Exam 2, option E defines a route with two route parameters and is therefore the correct answer. For completeness, the route parameters are **name** and **surname** which are sent back to the client that made the request separated by a space.

16.D - Objective 035.1

The **npm init** command is used to initialize a Node.js project: it will ask you a few questions (e.g. repository name, description, and so on) to generate a **package.json** file in your project route describing all the properties and dependencies of the project. Alternatively, you can accept all defaults using **npm init -y** or **npm init --yes**. Therefore, option D is the correct answer. For completeness, the **json, new**, and **build** commands do not exist for **npm**. Finally, remember that **npm init** can also be followed by an initializer which is an **npm** package, presumably used to create or update the **package.json** file and perform other initialization-related operations.

17. C - Objective 033.2

As explained in answer 9 of Practice Exam3, a pseudo-class is a keyword added to a selector that specifies a particular state of the selected elements. In particular, the **:hover** pseudo-class is used to indicate when the cursor (the mouse pointer) is over an element. Therefore, to set the background color of a paragraph in an HTML page to yellow when the mouse is over it, you can use **p:hover { background-color: yellow }**, making option C the correct answer. For completeness, the **onMouseOver** pseudo-class does not exist, while the **over.p**, **onMouseOver.p**, and **onHover.p** selectors are invalid.

18. C - Objective 032.2

To write **Hello World** in bold in your paragraph, you can use **<strong> Hello World </strong>** or **<b> Hello World </b>**. The difference is that **<strong>** is used to change the look of the text by also adding semantic importance (it gives more importance to a text, typically displaying the content in bold), while **<b>** only changes the presentation of the text without adding semantic importance (it only makes the text bold). **<strong>** is, in fact, a phrase tag, while **<b>** is a presentation tag. Therefore, option C is the correct answer. For completeness, the **<mark>** element is used to mark or highlight text in yellow, while the **<bold>** element does not exist.

19. C - Objective 033.4

The **clear** property is used to specify on which side of an HTML element floating elements cannot float so that the element is moved below the floating elements that precede it. In particular, you can use **left** to move an element below any floating element to the left that precedes it, **right** to move an element below any floating element to the right that precedes it, **both** to move an element below any floating element that precedes it, and **none** to not move an element below any floating element that precedes it. Therefore, option C is the correct answer. For completeness, the **br-float**, **cr-float**, and **skip** properties do not exist.

Answers to Practice Exam 4

20. C - Objective 034.3

According to the explanation of question 19 of Practice Exam 3, option C contains a valid **default** clause that can be set in a **switch** statement to perform a default action when no other matches occur and is therefore the correct answer.

21. B - Objective 035.2

In EJS, **views** is by default the folder in the application root directory where the template files are located. You can change this default directory to **custom** using **app.set('views', 'custom')**. Therefore, option B is the correct answer. For completeness, **app.set()** is used to assign a setting name to a value, while **app.use()** is used to mount a specified middleware function or functions at the specified path.

22. A - Objective 032.4

In HTML, the **<form>** element is used to create a document section containing interactive controls for user input such as the **<label>**, **<input>**, and **<button>** elements. In particular, the **action** attribute is used to specify where to send the form data when the form is submitted (the URL that processes the form submission) and the **method** attribute is used to specify the HTTP method used to send the form data (e.g. **get** or **post**). Therefore, option A is the correct answer. For completeness, the **<form>** element does not have the **submit**, **script**, **http**, and **type** attributes.

23. C - Objective 035.3

The **db.run()** method is used to execute an SQL statement with the specified parameters and then call a callback function (it does not retrieve any result data). Specifically, if you are passing parameters directly as method arguments or as an array, you need to use question marks (**?**) as placeholders for those parameters within the SQL statement to be executed. This makes option C the correct answer. For completeness, remember that you can also pass parameters as an object with named parameters (normally the properties of the object are the names of the fields prefixed with **$** whose value is passed to the SQL statement to be executed). Also remember that passing parameters allows you to sanitize the input preventing a common attack called SQL injection and that parameters cannot be used for column or table names.

24.B - Objective 034.2

According to the explanation of question 6 of Practice Exam 3, **number** is a primitive data type in JavaScript. This makes option B the correct answer.

25.C - Objective 032.3

According to the explanation of question 18 of Practice Exam 3, you need to specify a relative path. In particular, option A specifies a file located in the same folder as the HTML page, option B specifies a file located in the **img** folder in the directory where the HTML page is located, option C specifies a file located in the folder one level up from the directory where the HTML page is located (the directory above), and option D specifies a file located in the folder two levels up from the directory where the HTML page is located (two directories above). Therefore, option C is the correct answer.

26.B - Objective 032.3

The **href** attribute of an **<a>** element is used to specify the destination of a hyperlink. You can specify not only HTTP-based URLs, but also any other URL scheme supported by browsers such as **mailto:** for e-mail addresses and **tel:** for telephone numbers. This makes option B the correct answer.

27.A - Objective 031.3

Status code 200 indicates that the request has succeeded (its associate reason phrase is **OK**). For an HTTP GET request, this means that the resource has been fetched and transmitted in the message body. Therefore, option A is the correct answer. For completeness, status code 100 indicates that the client should continue the request or ignore the response if the request is already finished (its associate reason phrase is **Continue**), while 001 and A00 are not standard status codes.

28.B - Objective 034.4

The DOM method named **removeAttribute()** is used to remove the attribute with the name specified in round brackets from an element. Therefore, once you have selected the ordered list with **document.getElementById('list_id')**, you can use **removeAttribute('start')** to remove the **start** attribute from the list so that it starts at **1**. This makes option B the correct answer. For completeness, the **deleteAttribute()** method does not exist and the **start** property is invalid.

29.A - Objective 034.3

According to the explanation of question 36 of Practice Exam 1, you can use the **continue** instruction to terminate the execution of statements in the current iteration of a loop and start a new iteration. This makes option A the correct answer. For completeness, the **break** instruction is used to terminate the current loop, while the **next** and **jump** instructions do not exist in JavaScript.

30.D - Objective 033.3

The **text-decoration** property is a shorthand for: **text-decoration-line text-decoration-color text-decoration-style text-decoration-thickness**. In particular, **text-decoration-line** is used to set the type of text decoration (e.g. **underline, overline, line-through**, or **none**),

text-decoration-color is used to set the color of the text decoration (e.g. **yellow**, **rgb(255,0,0)**, or **#FFFFFF**), **text-decoration-style** is used to set the style of the text decoration (e.g. **solid**, **double**, or **dotted**), and **text-decoration-thickness** is used to set the thickness of the decoration line (e.g. **auto**, **5px**, or **15%**). Therefore, to accomplish the task of the question, you can set the two properties **text-decoration-line: line-through;** and **text-decoration-color: #FFFFFF;** or alternatively you can use the **text-decoration: line-through #FFFFFF;** property, making option D the correct answer (to specify white color, you can use **white**, **rgb(255,255,255)**, or **#FFFFFF**). For completeness, the **text-special** property does not exist and the hexadecimal value **#000000** represents the color black (to specify black color, you can also use **rgb(0,0,0)** or **black**).

31. C - Objective 031.3

The Etag (Entity Tag) field in the HTTP response header is used to specify an identifier for a particular version of a requested resource. It is used for cache validation (cache management is more efficient and bandwidth consumption is reduced) and to prevent simultaneous updates of resources. Using Etag, if a previously requested resource is not changed (its Etag value is the same as that of the cached version), when it is requested again, the server will not need to send a full response to the client which will then reuse the cached resource content. Therefore, the client will download the resource only if it changes, that is, if it has assigned a new Etag value (the cached resource needs to be updated). This makes option C the correct answer.

32. B - Objective 031.3

A Uniform Resource Locator (URL) is the address of a resource on the web. In particular, the URL specified in the question consists of five parts: **http** which is the scheme that specifies the protocol used by the browser to access the resource, **www.mysite.com** which is the

Answers to Practice Exam 4

domain name that indicates the web server on which the requested resource is stored and is separated from the scheme by **://**, **8080** which is the port used to access the resource on the web server separated from the domain name by a colon (**:**), **/test/user.html** which is the path to the resource on the Web server, and **f1=foo&f2=bar** which is the query string that is used to send small information to the server via the URL in the form of key-value pairs separated by an ampersand (**&**) and is separated from the path by a question mark (**?**). Therefore, the requested resource is **/test/user.html**, making option B the correct answer.

33. A, C, D - Objective 032.4

In HTML, an **<input>** element is used to specify an interactive control for a user interface where a user can enter data. The different types of **<input>** elements that can be displayed depend on the specified **type** attribute. For example, you can use **text** for a single-line text field (this is the default value), **date** for a control to insert a date (year, month, and day) with no time, **hidden** for a control that is not displayed but whose value is sent to the server, **radio** for a radio button, **checkbox** for a checkbox control, **reset** for a button that resets form fields to their default values, and **submit** for a button that submits the form. Therefore, options A, C, and D are the correct answers. For completeness, **select** and **form-submit** are invalid values for the **type** attribute.

34. A - Objective 034.2

The JavaScript code in the question defines an array of six elements: **array[0]=2**, **array[1]=5**, **array[2]=3**, **array[3]=7**, **array[4]=9**, and **array[5]=11** (array indexes start with 0). A new element is then added to the end of the array using the **push()** method (**array[6]=16**) and subsequently the last item (**array[6]**) is removed using the **pop()** method. As a result, the array will be the same as defined at the beginning and therefore **array[5]** will contain the value

11, which will be logged in the browser console. This makes option A the correct answer.

35. A - Objective 034.1

The **<script>** element is used to embed executable JavaScript code. You can write your own JavaScript statements inside this element as stated in answer 10 of Practice Exam 1 or specify an external source using the **src** attribute (it can be relative or absolute). In this second case, any code between the **<script>** and **</script>** tags is ignored. Therefore, option A is the correct answer. For completeness, the **<link>** element is used to specify the relationship between the current document and an external resource (typically a CSS style sheet) and does not have the **src** and **code** attributes, while the **<javascript>**, **<ext>**, and **<code-js>** elements do not exist.

36. D - Objective 033.3

The **border** property is used to set the border of an element and is a shorthand for: **border-width border-style border-color**. In particular, **border-width** is used to set the width of the border (e.g. **thin**, **medium**, or **thick**), **border-style** is used to set the style of the border (e.g. **solid**, **dotted**, or **double**), and **border-color** is used to set the color of the border (e.g. **blue**, **rgb(255,255,255)**, or **#FF0000** and if omitted, the color used is the color of the text). Each side of a border can be set individually using **border-top**, **border-right**, **border-bottom**, and **border-left** which are respectively a shorthand for **border-top-width border-top-style border-top-color**, **border-right-width border-right-style border-right-color**, **border-bottom-width border-bottom-style border-bottom-color**, and **border-left-width border-left-style border-left-color**. For **border-width**, **border-style**, and **border-color**, when one value is specified, it refers to all four sides, when two values are specified, the first refers to the top and bottom and the second to the left and right, when three values are specified, the first refers to the top, the second to the left and right, and the third to the bottom, and when four values are specified, they refer to the top, right, bottom, and left (so **border-width** is used to set the properties **border-top-width, border-right-width, border-bottom-width,** and **border-left-width** - **border-style** is used to set the properties **border-top-style, border-right-style, border-bottom-style,** and **border-left-style** - **border-color** is used to set the properties **border-top-color, border-right-color, border-bottom-color** and **border-left-color**). Therefore, to accomplish the task of the question, you can set the two properties **border-style: double; border-color: blue;** or alternatively you can use the **border: double blue;** property, making option D the correct answer. For completeness, the **border-line** and **set-border** properties do not exist.

37.A - Objective 034.3

The **if..else** statement allows you to perform an action based on the result of a conditional expression. Specifically, if the result is **true**, the code in the **true branch** is executed; otherwise the code in the **false branch** is executed. If you want to test multiple conditions, you need to combine them using logical operators. The code in the question checks whether the variable **a** is **undefined** or **null** (**==** treats **null** and **undefined** as the same as **null == undefined** evaluates to **true**) and if so, writes an error message to the browser console; otherwise it writes a success message. This makes option A the correct answer. For completeness, note that **undefined** is the value of a variable declared but not assigned a value, and that **null** is the value that can be assigned to a variable to indicate that it has no value (it means absence of a value).

38.B - Objective 035.3

Both the **db.all()** and **db.each()** methods are used to execute an SQL query with the specified parameters. The difference is that **db.all()** calls a callback function with an array containing all the results returned by the query, while **db.each()** calls a callback function for each row in the result set. This makes option B the correct answer. For completeness, the method that returns the first row matching the query is **db.get()**; this method then calls the callback function on the first result row.

39.C - Objective 034.3

According to the explanation of question 22 of Practice Exam 2, option C correctly creates a function with a function definition and is therefore the correct answer. For completeness, the **logmsg** function specified in the question simply logs a message with the current date in the browser console and has no parameters.

40.D - Objective 031.2

A web application is a computer program that is hosted on a remote server and usually runs on a browser to perform a certain activity over the Internet. It adopts the client/server model, that is, it has a client side and a server side, each of which performs different tasks based on the purpose of the application. In general, the client side of the application provides an interface to the client to make requests to the server, while the server side of the application processes and responds to the requests. A web application is not installed and access to local resources is mediated by the browser used to run it (user authorization is required). Finally, because a web application runs on a browser, it is multiplatform and independent of the operating system you are using it on; a web application usually works the same on any type of up-to-date browser. This makes option D the correct answer.